NATURAL CLEANING
Secrets

NATURAL CLEANING Secrets

EASY AND INEXPENSIVE SOLUTIONS FOR HOME, GARDEN, PETS, PERSONAL CARE AND MORE

Reader's Digest

NEW YORK/MONTREAL

A READER'S DIGEST BOOK

Copyright © 2022 Trusted Media Brands, Inc.

44 South Broadway

White Plains, NY 10601

ISBN 978-1-62145-799-2 (ppb)

ISBN 978-1-62145-800-5 (e-pub)

We are committed to both the quality of our products and the service we provide to our customers. We value your comments, so please feel free to contact us at TMBBookTeam@TrustedMediaBrands.com.

For more *Reader's Digest* products and information, visit our website:

www.rd.com (in the United States)

www.readersdigest.ca (in Canada)

Printed in China

10 9 8 7 6 5 4 3 2 1

Cover and interior illustration: Kat Chadwick; accent leaves: Natalia Kuprova/Getty Images; take care burst: LesyaD/Getty Images.

NOTE TO OUR READERS

The information in this book should not be substituted for, or used to alter, medical therapy without your doctor's advice. For a specific health problem, consult your physician for guidance.

This publication contains the opinions and ideas of its contributors and is designed to provide useful information to the reader on the subject matter covered. This publication is sold with the understanding that the contributors and the publisher are not engaged in rendering legal advice. Laws vary from state to state, and readers with specific issues should seek the services of an attorney. Any references in this publication to any products or services do not constitute or imply an endorsement or recommendation. The publisher and the contributors specifically disclaim any responsibility for any liability, loss, or risk (personal, financial or otherwise) that may be claimed or incurred as a consequence, directly or indirectly, of the use and/or application of any of the contents of this publication.

CONTENTS

CLEANING DYNAMIC DUO

THERE IS GROWING CONCERN over the toxicity of many common commercial cleaning agents. This has led to increased interest in familiar agents such as vinegar, baking soda, borax, etc. It has also led to the development of new technologies allowing general cleaning to be done with just plain water or some form of empowered water. Coupled with microfiber cloths and mops, these are truly helping to create healthier environments for us all.

Microfibers represent the biggest change in cleaning since the introduction of detergents in the 1950s. Because they are made from nylon and polyester, it can be argued that microfibers cannot be considered green or natural. However, they can reduce or eliminate the use of cleaning chemicals, require less water to clean, and waste fewer paper products. They are also durable tools, as some can be laundered several hundred times. In studies at the University of California, Davis, microfibers removed 99% of the soil and germs from hard surfaces using just water versus 33% removal using conventional cotton. Some of the best microfibers have lab tests showing a removal rate of 99.99% for tested bacteria when paired with just plain water. Coupled with deionized water, they make an even more powerful cleaning combination.

Deionized water is pure water with all minerals removed. Our cleaning service does over 500 residential cleans per month with high-grade microfibers using deionized water as our general cleaner. If deionized is unavailable, distilled water can be a close second. This is water that has been boiled into vapor and condensed back into liquid to remove contaminants.

When you choose cleaning methods from this book, I recommend trying this dynamic cleaning duo for most tasks. But know that you will need extra oomph on jobs such as heavy grease and hard-water scale. Look inside for great ways to tackle cleaning with baking soda for grease, and vinegar for soap scum or hard-water scale, and much, much more.

—**Bruce Vance,** *co-owner*
Town & Country Cleaning Services

About This Book

READY, SET, CLEAN! You've just found the earth-friendly way to keep a home fresh and tidy for less time and money.

The secrets throughout this book show you how to get more bang for your buck from everyday items you probably already own. You'll be amazed by how much you can accomplish using just a few of the most versatile of these items, such as baking soda, salt, vinegar or a lemon.

There are also many tangible benefits to making common household products on your own:

+ In many cases, the quality of the homemade product is superior to the equivalent store-bought item.
+ You'll save money.
+ You know exactly what goes into it.
+ You can adjust the recipe to meet your own needs or preferences.
+ You're creating less waste by avoiding extra packaging and by using repurposed bottles and cloths, so you can feel good about doing your bit to help the environment.
+ And the best part is that everything here is natural!

Start slowly and use these methods and recipes in small areas first to make sure they work for you or with your materials or items. Also, be aware that though many of these agents are found in nature and are minimally processed, it doesn't mean you can throw caution aside. "Natural" does not equal "safe" and "nontoxic." Always work in well-ventilated areas, wear gloves and goggles when appropriate, and be aware of the presence of children and pets around agents such as borax.

We wish you happy and healthy cleaning!

—The Editors of *Reader's Digest*

IN THE
KITCHEN

HAND-WASH DISHES

DIY DISHWASHING LIQUID

An inexpensive recipe for washing by hand that gets your dishes clean.

¼ cup (60 ml) pure soap flakes
1½ cups (375 ml) hot water
¼ cup (60 ml) glycerin
½ tsp. (2.5 ml) lemon oil
1 clean 16-oz. (500 ml) repurposed squirt bottle

If you are unable to find pure soap flakes, lightly grate a bar of pure soap on a coarse kitchen grater to measure ¼ cup (60 ml).

In a medium jug, pour soap flakes into hot water and stir with a fork until most of the soap has dissolved. Let solution cool for 5 minutes.

Stir in the glycerin and lemon oil. A loose gel will form as it cools. Use the fork to break up any congealed parts, and pour the liquid into bottle. Use 2 to 3 teaspoons (10 to 15 ml) per sink of hot water to clean dishes.

THE POWER OF AN OLD-FASHIONED SCRUB

Save a few bucks on your electric bill and get super-clean dishes in the process. Fill your sink with warm water, add a few squirts of natural dish soap, pull on rubber gloves and have at it. If your dishes are really a mess, let them soak for 10 minutes in lemon juice-infused hot water; if they're still sticky, sprinkle them with kosher salt and dish soap before rinsing them until they're squeaky clean.

AIR DRY FOR BEST RESULTS

Place dishes vertically in a dish drainer. Make sure the handles of stainless steel cutlery and silverware all point down.

Insider Tip

Dry dishes while they are still warm to prevent watermarks and to bring out the shine. Use dish towels made from an absorbent material, such as cotton or linen, and wash them several times before first use.

CLEAR UP CLOUDY GLASS

Ovenproof casserole dishes of clear glass may be marred with large cloudy spots even though they're clean as a whistle.

Eggs, milk, cheese and other proteins are the culprits, and none can stand up to white vinegar. All that removal takes is rubbing the spots with a vinegar-soaked sponge or cleaning cloth.

REMOVE LIPSTICK FROM DISHES

When you're washing dishes, rub lipstick marks with salt to make the marks much easier to wash off.

LIFT COFFEE AND TEA STAINS FROM CHINA

Don't let those annoying coffee or tea stains on your good china spoil another special occasion. Remove them by dipping a moist cloth into baking soda to form a stiff paste and gently rub

the paste on your cups and saucers. Rinse clean and then dry. Or try removing a tea stain or residue from a porcelain cup by mixing hot water with 1 teaspoon (5 ml) baking soda in the cup, letting it soak, then washing it out thoroughly.

MAKING SOFT SOAP

Soap making is an age-old tradition, and this recipe has been used for generations. A teaspoon (5 ml) of gel will clean the dishes— but don't use it in the dishwasher.

- 6 Tbsp. (90 ml) finely grated unscented bar soap
- 1 qt. (1 L) cold water
- 1 heatproof 1-qt. (1 L) jar with tight-fitting lid

Put the finely grated soap in an old saucepan.

Add the water and place the saucepan over low heat. Bring just to a boil, stirring occasionally, then simmer gently for 15 minutes.

Pour into the jar, let cool, then seal and leave for a day to form a gel.

GET RID OF MINERAL DEPOSITS

Light mineral deposits are easy to wipe off porcelain with a damp sponge and vinegar. For containers, pour a dash of citric acid and hot water into the container and let it sit for 1 hour. Repeat as needed until the residue is dissolved, then wash and rinse thoroughly.

WASHING WOOD

Wash wooden handles promptly and allow them to dry naturally. Occasionally rub in some olive oil and wipe off any excess with a clean cloth or paper towel.

HOW TO CLEAN SCISSORS

It's best not to clean good kitchen shears in water because it can rust the central fastener and dull the blades. Instead, dip a cloth in undiluted white vinegar and wipe the blades well. Dry with a towel.

BOOST POTENCY OF DISHWASHING LIQUID

Only one squeeze of dishwashing liquid left? Add it to a dishpan partially filled with hot water, then stir in 1 to 2 tablespoons (15 to 30 ml) baking soda while allowing more hot water to run. The water won't look as bubbly but it

Metal Utensils

Practice special care when cleaning metal kitchen tools, which can be sharp and can get rusty.

Clean metal flour sieves immediately after use in cold water—warm water will make the flour stick like glue.

Use an old hard-bristled toothbrush to clean cheese (or lemon zest or anything else) from a cheese grater or garlic press. Scrub the grater with the wet toothbrush, then rinse the grater and the toothbrush and you're done. No muss, no fuss, and you haven't destroyed a sponge or cloth in the process.

If metal gets rusty, sprinkle it with salt and rub with bacon rind.

will feel soapy. As you wash, you'll notice that grease disappears and that baked-on food comes off easily.

BLENDER SOLUTION

Forget about taking your blender apart to wash it thoroughly. Instead, fill it partway with warm water and dishwashing detergent, cover it, and run it for a few seconds. Empty it, rinse it, air-dry it and call it a day.

CLEANSE BABY BOTTLES AND ACCESSORIES

Here's some great advice for new parents. Keep all your baby bottles, nipples, caps and brushes "baby fresh" by soaking them overnight in a container filled with hot water and half a box of baking soda. Make sure you give everything a good rinsing afterward, and dry thoroughly before using. Baby bottles can also be boiled in a full pot of water and 3 tablespoons (45 ml) baking soda for 3 minutes.

GLASSWARE

Handy Hack

To keep cold glasses from cracking, wash them in warm water only. Scalding hot water will leach the shine from crystal glasses and dull the gold or silver rims on glassware.

LEAVE LINT BEHIND

Dry glasses with a linen dish towel to avoid leaving lint flecks.

Insider Tip

Place a dish towel in the sink when washing delicate glassware to prevent chipping.

NO-SPOTS GLASSWARE

To prevent spotting on glass pitchers, candlesticks, drinking glasses, and any other everyday or special occasion glassware, soak a piece for 3 to 4 minutes in a bath of 2 gallons (8 L) water and ½ cup (125 ml) white vinegar. Shake off any water droplets, and then dry and polish the piece with a clean soft cloth.

Take Care

Rinse beer, wine and champagne glasses with warm, clear water only. Detergent residue can change the taste of a drink as well as take the fizz out of champagne and the head off your beer.

REMOVE INVISIBLE FILM

Though drinking glasses, mugs, plates and bowls might look clean after a washing, they could still be covered with a thin film of grease, invisible to the naked eye. See for yourself by making a thin paste of baking soda and water, dipping a sponge into it, and rubbing the glass or china surface well. Rinse and dry with a soft cloth, and dishes may sparkle as never before and even feel different.

HOW TO TREAT CRYSTAL

If residue dries inside a crystal pitcher that won't tolerate hard scrubbing without being scratched, fill it with a mixture of 2 parts strong black tea and 1 part white vinegar. After it sits overnight, discard the solution and wash the pitcher with a soft cloth dipped in soapy water.

CLEANING ETCHED CRYSTAL

With deeply etched crystal, use an old-fashioned shaving brush or large makeup brush to work soapy water into crevices at cleaning time. These brushes are rigid enough to root out dirt without scratching. Rinse under running water.

SMOOTH NICKS AND SCRATCHES

If you notice a small nick on the edge of a drinking glass, use an emery board to smooth it out. To eliminate a scratch, rub it out with non-gel white toothpaste on a soft cloth, then rinse. The mildly abrasive toothpaste will smooth the glass just enough to make the scratch invisible.

GOT DISCOLORED GLASS?

Did your dishwasher fail to remove those stubborn stains from your glassware? Hand-scrubbing failed, too? Try mixing a handful of salt in a quart (1 L) of vinegar and soak the glassware overnight. Stains should wipe off by morning.

 Insider Tip Store wine glasses upright. There is a risk that the rims could be damaged if the glasses stick to the cabinet shelf. Also, the glasses could develop a musty smell.

USE A BOTTLE BRUSH

Clean narrow-neck glass containers with a bottle brush using vinegar and water for mineral deposits or soap buildup, and baking soda for oily residues.

EGGSHELL TIP FOR A DECANTER

Remove hard-to-reach dirt in a decanter or container with crumbled eggshells and lemon juice. Let it stand two days, shake it back and forth a few times, then rinse.

Quick Guide: Cleaning China, Crystal and Glassware

Put the sparkle back in your glassware by adding vinegar to your rinse water or dishwater.

To keep everyday glassware gleaming, add ¼ cup (60 ml) vinegar to your dishwasher's rinse cycle.

To rid drinking glasses of cloudiness or spots caused by hard water, heat up a pot of equal parts white vinegar and water (use full-strength vinegar if your glasses are very cloudy), and let them soak in it for 15 to 30 minutes. Give them a good scrubbing with a bottle brush and rinse clean.

Add 2 tablespoons (30 ml) vinegar to the dishwater when you're cleaning your good crystal glasses. Rinse them in a solution of 3 parts warm water to 1 part vinegar and allow them to air-dry. You can also wash delicate crystal and fine china by adding 1 cup (250 ml) vinegar to a basin of warm water. Gently dunk the glasses into the solution and allow them to dry.

To get coffee stains and other discolorations off china dishes and teacups, try scrubbing them with equal parts vinegar and salt, followed by rinsing them under warm water.

CONTAINERS

SMELLS, BEGONE!

You can eliminate smells from plastic containers. After washing and drying them well, fill them with crumpled newspaper or coffee grounds and freeze them overnight.

TIPS FOR PLASTIC CONTAINERS

Another method to remove foul odor from a plastic container is to pour a little tomato juice on a sponge and wipe it around the inside of the container. Wash the container and lid in warm, soapy water, dry well, and store them separated in the freezer for a couple of days. The container will be stench-free and ready to use again.

DEODORIZE BOTTLES FOR REUSE

You'd like to reuse those wonderful wide-mouthed pickle jars, but simply washing them with soap and water doesn't get rid of the pickle smell. What to do? Add 1 teaspoon (5 ml) dry mustard to a quart (1 L) of water, fill the jar and let it soak overnight. It'll smell fresh by morning. This solution also banishes the odor of tomatoes, garlic and other foods with strong scents.

REMOVE THERMOS RESIDUE

To remove residue on the inside of a thermos and to get it smelling fresh again, mix ¼ cup (60 ml) baking soda in 4 cups (1 L) water. Fill the thermos with the solution—if necessary, give it a going-over with a bottle brush to loosen things up. Let it soak overnight and rinse clean before using.

TO PREVENT A SMELLY THERMOS

Keep a thermos fresh by placing a whole clove inside the thermos flask before capping it for storage. A teaspoon of salt works well, too. Make sure you empty and rinse the thermos before using it.

COFFEE AND TEA

REFRESH A DRIP-FILTER COFFEE MAKER

If your coffee consistently comes out weak or bitter, odds are your drip coffee maker needs cleaning. Fill the decanter with 2 cups (500 ml) white vinegar and 1 cup (250 ml) water. Place a filter in the machine and pour the solution into the coffee maker's water chamber. Turn on the coffee maker and let it run through a full brew cycle. Remove the filter and replace it with a fresh one. Then run clean water through the machine for two full cycles, replacing the filter again for the second brew. If you have soft water, clean your coffee maker after 80 brew cycles. If you have hard water, clean it after 40 brew cycles.

CLEAN AN AUTOMATIC COFFEE MAKER

Caring for your automatic coffee maker means never having to worry about bitter or weak coffee. Every two weeks or so, brew a pot of 4 cups (1 L) water mixed with ¼ cup (60 ml) baking soda, followed by a pot of clean water. Sweeten your coffee maker's plastic basket by using an old toothbrush to give it an occasional scrubbing with a paste of 2 tablespoons (30 ml) baking soda and 1 tablespoon (15 ml) water.

Rinse thoroughly with cold water when you're done.

PERCOLATOR MAINTENANCE

If your percolated coffee tastes a bit bitter these days, try this. Fill the percolator with water, add ¼ cup (60 ml) salt and percolate as usual. Rinse the percolator and all its parts well, and the next pot should have the delicious flavor you love.

Handy Hack

Hold the spices! If you ever use your coffee grinder to grind spices, be sure to clean all the remnants out of the grinder before switching back to coffee beans. How to go about it? Simply grind two or three slices of cut-up, plain white bread in the machine.

PURGE STAINS FROM A CARAFE

Over time, caffeine will discolor the glass carafe of your automatic coffee maker, but you can easily make it look like new. Fill the carafe one quarter full with water. Cut a lemon into four wedges, squeeze the juice of two of them into the water and drop all four lemon wedges into the

Rice to the Rescue

Use this simple grocery item you likely have around the house to help keep your coffeepot and grinder clean.

Clean a glass coffeepot by adding a handful of uncooked rice and filling it with dishwater. Put the lid on and shake until stains are gone.

De-bitter your coffee grinder with rice. When you grind your own coffee beans, it's almost impossible to brush all of the residue out of the grinder when you're done—and accumulated residue can make coffee taste bitter. To get rid of the residue, run a cup of raw white rice through the grinder once every month. The rice will clean the grinder and sharpen the blades at the same time.

carafe. Add 2 tablespoons (30 ml) salt and swirl the carafe around for 2 to 3 minutes. Empty the carafe and scrub the inside with soapy water. Rinse, dry and return the crystal-clear carafe to its base.

BRUSH AWAY ESPRESSO

If you're a fan of espresso, you're also familiar with how finely ground Italy's favorite coffee is. To keep it from clogging the filter screen on your espresso maker, scrub the screen gently after each use with a soft toothbrush. If any bits remain, remove them with a straight pin.

USE HOT WATER

Never wash teapots with dishwashing liquid or in the dishwasher; use just hot water. A layer of tannin residue actually enhances the aroma of the tea. However, if you don't like the look of the tannin, remove it gently by adding vinegar to the teapot and let it steep before rinsing it out. Another option is to dip a damp cloth into baking soda and use this to wipe out the pot before rinsing it.

SHINE YOUR TEAPOT SPOUT

Teapots with seriously stained spouts can be cleaned with salt. Stuff the spout with salt and let it sit overnight or at least several hours. Then run boiling water through the pot, washing away the salt and revealing the old sparkle. If the stain persists, treat the rim with a cotton swab dipped in salt.

ERASE TEA AND COFFEE STAINS

Tea and coffee leave stains on cups and in pots. You can easily scrub away these unattractive rings by sprinkling salt on a sponge and rubbing in little circles across the ring. If the stain persists, mix white vinegar with salt in equal proportions and rub with a sponge.

Cleaning a Kettle

Removing water deposits from your kettle not only will make tea and coffee taste better, it will also help save electricity.

Various products are available at stores but water and vinegar or citric acid (a gentler option) will do the job, too. Fill the kettle halfway with equal parts water and vinegar, or halfway with water plus about 2 tablespoons (30 ml) citric acid, and bring to a boil. Let the solution work for a few hours before rinsing out the kettle thoroughly.

Another effective way to clean the kettle is to use lemon juice and baking soda.

Placing a pebble or marble chip in the kettle can help prevent the buildup of minerals.

POTS, PANS AND COOKWARE

POT FREEZE HACK

If your favorite pot has been left on the stove too long, you have a burned-on mess to contend with. All you have to do is to place the pot in the freezer for a couple of hours. When the burned-on food freezes, it will be easier to remove.

DRIED? LET IT SOAK

Dried food is easier to remove if you let it soak overnight in water with a little salt added. The next day, put the pan on the stove and bring the water to a boil. Allow it to cool, and the residue should wipe out easily. To finish, wash with dishwashing liquid.

REMOVE BAKED-ON FOOD

Yes, you can remove food that has been baked onto cooking pans or serving plates. In fact, it's easy. Baked-on food can be "lifted" with a pretreatment of salt. Before washing, sprinkle the stuck-on food with salt. Dampen the area, let it sit until the salt lifts the baked-on food, then wash it away with soapy water.

SCRUB OFF BURNED MILK

Burned milk is one of the toughest stains to remove, but salt makes this cleanup a lot easier. Wet the burned pan and sprinkle it with salt. Wait about 10 minutes, then scrub the pan. The salt also absorbs that burned-milk odor. Cleaned pot, vanished odor.

MAKE AN ALL-PURPOSE SCRUB FOR POTS AND PANS

How would you like an effective scouring mix that costs a few pennies and can be safely used on all of your metal cookware—including expensive copper pots and pans? Want even better news? You probably already have this "miracle mix" in your kitchen. Simply combine equal parts salt and flour and add just enough vinegar to make a paste. Work the paste around the cooking surface and the outside of the utensil, and rinse off with warm water. Dry thoroughly with a soft dish towel.

SHINE ALUMINUM COOKWARE

Aluminum pots conduct heat beautifully, but woe to the cook who lets acid touch the pan: Aluminum discolors like crazy.

Remove discoloration and stains by putting 1 quart (1 L) water and 2 tablespoons (30 ml) cream of tartar in the pan. Bring to a boil, and as it simmers for 10 minutes, stains fade and disappear.

CARE FOR ALUMINUM COOKWARE

Do not use washing soda (sodium carbonate) to clean aluminum cookware, and never put it in the dishwasher. One of the best ways to clean aluminum ware is with soapy water and steel wool. To make steel wool last longer, wrap it in a piece of aluminum foil.

Take Care Never use a wire scourer or steel wool on an aluminum-lined copper pan, as this will absolutely destroy the lining.

QUICK CAST-IRON CLEANUP

Food tastes delicious when it's cooked in cast iron, but cleaning those heavy pots and pans isn't much fun. You can make the cleanup a lot easier by pouring some club soda into the cookware while it's still warm. The bubbly soda will prevent the mess from sticking.

A CAST-IRON DO

Rub vegetable oil on the inside of a cast-iron skillet to keep it seasoned—and do it after each wash and any other time you please.

Take Care Soaking a cast-iron skillet in soapy water can deplete the fat that seeps into the porous surface and seasons the skillet—and an unseasoned skillet is a recipe for frustration. You'll be contending with food that sticks and burns and seems almost impossible to clean off.

CHOICE CAST-IRON CLEANERS

Both coarse salt and borax (sodium borate) are more cast-iron-friendly than dishwashing detergents, so use either to get burned food off a treasured pan that may have been passed down from your grandmother. Just sprinkle the crystals into the pan and scrub with a wet sponge or paper towel. Then rinse with fresh cold water and dry immediately (cast iron is quick to rust).

NO STICK, NO RUST, NO KIDDING!

They call it nonstick, but stuff stuck. And your beloved cast-iron skillet has rust stains. Scrub the spots with a damp sponge sprinkled with baking soda. Make sure to wet the sponge well to dissolve the baking soda and avoid scratching your nonstick. Citric acid, which occurs naturally in lemons, is another effective rust remover. Mix 1 tablespoon (15 ml) citric acid with 2 cups (500 ml) water. Dip a scrubbing brush into the solution and scrub the rust spots away. To finish, wash the item as you normally would.

Take Care To prevent cast-iron cookware from rusting, store it in a cupboard away from cooking vapors.

RHUBARB TO THE RESCUE

When rhubarb is in season, save the trimmings from rhubarb stalks and boil them to remove deposits from the surface of enamel cookware. Rinse thoroughly afterward.

Take Care Never pour cold water into a hot enamel pan— it could cause the enamel to crack or flake away from the surface.

SOAK STAINS OFF ENAMEL PANS

You can run out of elbow grease trying to scrub burned-on stains from enamel pans. Skip the sweat. Soak the pan overnight in salt water, then boil salt water in the pan the next day. The stains should lift right off. If it is just a stain, try soaking enamelware overnight in a strong solution of washing soda (sodium carbonate).

CLEANSE GREASY IRON PANS

Because grease is not water-soluble, it can be tough to remove from iron pans. Take a shortcut by sprinkling salt in the pan before you wash it. The salt will absorb most of the grease. Wipe the pan out and wash as usual.

FOR NONSTICK PANS

Clean nonstick pans with water and dishwashing liquid. Finish by coating the surface with a drop of cooking oil.

REMOVE STAINS FROM NONSTICK COOKWARE

It may be called nonstick cookware, but a few of those stains seem to be stuck on pretty well. Blast them away by boiling 1 cup (250 ml) water mixed with 2 tablespoons (30 ml) baking soda and ½ cup (125 ml) vinegar for 10 minutes. Wash in hot, soapy water, rinse well and allow to dry. Season with a bit of olive oil.

POLISH COPPER AND BRASS

Put the shimmer back in your brass, bronze and copper objects by making a paste of equal parts white vinegar and salt, or vinegar and baking soda (wait for the fizzing to stop before using). Use a clean, soft cloth or paper towel to rub the paste into the item until the tarnish is gone. Then rinse with cool water and polish with a soft towel until dry.

4 Ways to Clean Copper Pots

Copper cookware is beautiful—and it darn well should be, considering what it costs. To keep it looking like all it's worth, try these out-of-the-ordinary cleansers.

1. Salt and vinegar Fill a repurposed spray bottle with vinegar and 3 tablespoons (45 ml) salt, shake until salt dissolves, and give the copper a spray. Let the pots sit for 10 to 12 minutes and then scrub clean.

2. Lemon juice and cream of tartar Mix these into a paste that's thin enough to spread but thick enough to cling. Apply to copperware with a clean cloth, and let it stand for 5 minutes before washing with warm water.

3. Worcestershire sauce Yep, you heard right. Soak a sponge with the sauce and rub it over the surface of copper pots and pans. Let it sit 1 to 2 minutes and then wipe clean. Rinse well and dry.

4. Half a lemon and salt If you find stubborn tarnish spots on your copperware, dip lemon halves in salt and rub the pesky stains away.

USE TOOTHPASTE ON STAINLESS COOKWARE

Fingerprints all over your sparkling-new stainless cookware? Dampen it with lukewarm water, apply an inch (2.5 cm) of low-abrasion toothpaste and brush away those unsightly marks. Rinse, dry and ogle that new shiny cookware again.

SPINACH IS YOUR NATURAL CLEANING FRIEND

Cooking spinach in a stainless steel pan will kill two birds with one stone. Not only will you have a healthy serving of greens, you will also restore the shine to your pan. The oxalic acid in spinach will give the steel a thorough cleaning. Using oxalic-acid-rich rhubarb will give you the same result.

TRY POTATO RUST REMOVER ON TIN PANS

Tin pie plates and other kitchen utensils are subject to rust if they are not dried carefully after each washing. For little more than the price of a potato, restore tinware without harsh chemicals. Peel a potato and cut it into easy-to-handle pieces. Put some baking soda or salt in a saucer. Then dip a cut piece of potato in the soda or salt, and rub it over the rust spots. Rinse the tin utensil and dry thoroughly.

TOOTHBRUSH FOR A WAFFLE IRON

A clean, soft toothbrush is just the right utensil to clean crumbs and burned batter from the nooks and crannies of a waffle iron. Use it to spread oil evenly on the waffle iron surface before next use, too.

RECIPE: HOMEMADE SCRUB POWDER

Use this mixture to scrub grease and grime from your stainless steel and enameled cookware. (If you use baking soda on aluminum cookware, it may cause darkening.)

2½	cups (625 ml) baking soda
1½	cups (375 ml) salt
2	Tbsp. (30 ml) cream of tartar
1	clean 32-oz. (1 L) container with lid

Mix all the ingredients together well, and store in a tightly sealed container.

To use, pour 2 to 3 tablespoons (30 to 45 ml) powder onto cookware and scrub with a brush or nylon scrubber that's been slightly moistened with water. Rinse well; dry with a soft cloth.

SINKS

GARDEN LIME DOES THE TRICK

There's no need to use a special cleaning product on a stainless steel sink. A mix of powdered garden lime and an inexpensive liquid soap is an environmentally friendly alternative. Apply with a sponge scourer.

BUFF UP A STAINLESS STEEL SINK

Metal sinks look terrific when they go in, but the impact of daily use steadily dulls their luster until they look stained and worn. Bring the shine back to a steel sink by drying it with a dish towel. Then sprinkle plain white flour over the surface—not too much, just a light coating—and rub it with a soft dry cloth. Rinse with warm water and polish with another dry cloth.

SHINE STAINLESS STEEL AND CHROME TRIM

Another option to put the shine back in a stainless steel sink is to sprinkle it with baking soda and give it a rubdown—moving in the direction of the grain—with a moist cloth. To polish dull chrome trim on your appliances, pour a bit of baking soda on a damp sponge and rub over the chrome. Let it dry for an hour or so, then wipe it down with warm water and dry with a clean cloth.

RUB OUT HEAVY SINK STAINS

Get rid of those stubborn stains—even rust—in your stainless steel or porcelain sink. Make a paste of 1 cup (250 ml) borax and ¼ cup (60 ml) lemon juice. Put some of the paste on a cloth or sponge, rub it into the stain and rinse with running warm water. The stain should wash away.

A SIMPLE ANSWER FOR DISCOLORATION

Use a couple of dashes of lemon juice on a sponge to rub down a discolored sink.

GOT A POTATO?

Rubbing stainless steel sinks with a cut raw potato or potato peelings is another proven way to remove stains.

SCORCHED SINK

Rub out heat marks in a sink by sprinkling on a little baking soda, then rinsing it off.

VANISHING ACT

Spots from mineral deposits disappear when you treat them with a mixture of vinegar and salt. Place a paper towel over the spot, sprinkle with the solution and let it sit. Remove the paper towel and rinse.

SPEED UP A DRAIN

Kitchen sink starting to drain slowly? You probably have a clog waiting to happen. Make sure it never does by slowly pouring a whole 2-liter bottle of cola down the drain. The potent carbonic acid in cola will get things moving again.

Take Care If you use a method involving vinegar to help unclog a drain, never use it after trying a commercial drain cleaner; the cleaner could react with vinegar to create dangerous fumes.

Natural Drain Solutions

The combination of vinegar and baking soda is one of the most effective mixtures for unclogging and deodorizing drains. It's also far gentler on your pipes than commercial drain cleaners.

To clear clogs in sink and tub drains, use a funnel to pour in ½ cup (125 ml) baking soda followed by 1 cup (250 ml) vinegar. When the foaming subsides, flush with hot tap water. Wait 5 minutes and flush again with cold water.

Besides clearing blockages, this technique also washes away odor-causing bacteria.

To speed up a slow drain, pour in ½ cup (125 ml) salt followed by 2 cups (500 ml) boiling vinegar. Flush with hot and cold water.

DEODORIZE YOUR KITCHEN SINK

Here's an incredibly easy way to keep your sink drain sanitized and smelling clean. Mix equal parts water and vinegar in a bowl, pour the solution into an ice cube tray, and freeze it. Then simply drop a couple of "vinegar cubes" into the sink every week or so, let them melt into the drain, and follow with a cold-water rinse.

SANITIZE YOUR SINK

Germs can hang around in your sink on microscopic food particles. To kill them off, fill a spray bottle with full-strength rubbing alcohol. After you finish washing dishes, spray the sink with alcohol and then rub it down with a clean dish towel or paper towel.

TEA THYME FOR PORCELAIN

Charming though they are, porcelain sinks are hard to clean because abrasive cleaners dull (and often scratch) porcelain surfaces. Take the gentle route and clean your sink with fresh lemon thyme tea. Place four to five bunches of fresh lemon thyme in a 3-gallon (12 L) metal bucket and fill it with boiling water. Steep for 5 to 6 hours and strain. Stop up the sink, pour in the tea and let it sit overnight. When you drain it the next morning, you'll find a gleaming white sink that smells fresh.

DISPOSAL DEODORIZERS

Garbage disposal units are self-cleaning, but they can get smelly. To keep them running smoothly, operate with a full stream of running cold water that will flush the ground-up debris away. To keep unpleasant smells from wafting out of your disposal, try grinding citrus peels—lemon, lime, orange or grapefruit. A couple of bunches of fresh mint will also do the trick.

ICE-COLD DISPOSAL DEGREASER

Degrease your garbage disposal by occasionally grinding five or six ice cubes with ½ cup (125 ml) baking soda. The ice congeals the grease, priming it for attack by the fast-acting sodium bicarbonate and sending it down the drain. To flush out any residue, fill the stoppered sink with 2 to 3 inches (5 to 8 cm) hot water and run the water through the disposal.

DISHWASHER

WASH OUT YOUR APPLIANCE

To remove built-up soap film in your dishwasher, pour 1 cup (250 ml) undiluted white vinegar into the bottom of the unit—or in a bowl on the top rack. Then run the machine through a full cycle without any dishes or detergent. Do this once a month, especially if you live in a hard-water area. However, if there's no mention of vinegar in your dishwasher owner's manual, check with the manufacturer first. Also, remember to clean the filters.

TRY A DEEP CLEAN

Faintly funky smell in the dishwasher? Sort it out fast with a baking soda wash. Put 1 cup (250 ml) baking soda in the bottom of the dishwasher and run it on a rinse cycle. If the smell persists, sprinkle a few tablespoons (30 to 45 ml) on the bottom of the washer to sit there between loads. There's no need to rinse it out before running the next load. Or, add a few drops of concentrated orange oil during the next wash cycle.

GET A JUMP ON ODORS

If you are looking for a way to keep odors out of your dishwasher in the first place, just add ½ cup (125 ml) lemon juice to the detergent receptacle each time you use the machine. Lemon is a natural deodorizer and degreaser.

GOING ON VACATION?

If you are not using your dishwasher for a period, sprinkle a few tablespoons of baking soda in the bottom to absorb bad smells. It will simply rinse away the first time you use your machine again.

Handy Hack

Don't overdo it on dishwashing detergent. Dishwashers use less water than they did in days gone by, and detergents are more concentrated. This means you need less soap. Otherwise, not only are you spending more than you have to on something that's (literally) going down the drain—but also, too much soap leads to cloudy glasses.

FAST, CHEAP RINSING AGENT

Here's an easy way to get those dishes sparkling in your dishwasher without using any chemical rinsing agents. Just stop the dishwasher during its rinse cycle and add 1 to 1½ cups (250 to 375 ml) white vinegar. Or pour the vinegar into the rinse compartment beforehand (being careful not to overfill). Then wash the dishes as usual.

CLIP OUT SPRAY-ARM DEBRIS

If your dishwasher seems to have fallen down on the job lately, the spray arms could be clogged. Open the washer and take a peek at the top of the three-pronged spray arms to see if the holes look clogged. Test for clogging by sticking a wooden toothpick into one of the holes; if it shows signs of dirt when it's pulled out, the holes need cleaning. Unfasten the clips or screws holding the spray arms in place and put the arms in the kitchen sink. Then unbend a paper clip and insert the long end into each spray hole, moving it around to dislodge the blockage. Finish the job by rinsing the spray arms under the faucet and fastening them back in their proper places.

REMOVE DISHWASHER RUST STAINS

If you have hard water, the inside of your dishwasher will eventually get dingy as iron and other minerals build up on the interior walls. Return your appliance to pristine condition by putting a package of lemonade Kool-Aid in the soap dispenser, then running

a hot (or "heavy") cycle. The inside will gleam like new again.

Take Care Don't put wooden cooking utensils or pots and pans with wooden (or plastic) handles in the dishwasher. The wood will swell up and eventually it will be ruined.

DIY AUTOMATIC DISHWASHER DETERGENT

Even if you live in a hard-water area, this simple, inexpensive detergent recipe will help keep your dishes shiny and spotless.

- 2 **cups (500 ml) borax**
- 2 **cups (500 ml) washing soda**
- 1 **clean 32-oz. (1 L) container with cover**

Combine the borax and washing soda in the container and seal it tightly for storage.

For each load of dishes, put 2 tablespoons (30 ml) mixture in the dishwasher soap dispenser.

OVEN AND STOVETOP

BASIC OVEN CLEANER

Try this odorless recipe the next time you need to clean your oven, and leave those caustic chemical-based oven cleaners where they belong—on the store shelf.

2   Tbsp. (30 ml) liquid soap
2   tsp. (10 ml) borax
1   clean 16-oz. (500 ml) repurposed spray bottle
2   cups (500 ml) warm water
½   cup (125 ml) baking soda in an open bowl

Pour the soap and borax into the spray bottle and add the warm water. Shake well to dissolve the borax.

Spray the solution on the oven's surfaces, giving special attention to dried, cooked-on spills.

Let the sprayed mixture sit for 30 minutes to 1 hour, then scrub the oven surfaces with a damp scrub pad dipped in the baking soda. Rinse with clean water.

Handy Hack If you have a dish that may overflow (such as a fruit pie baked on a flat tray), line the bottom of the oven with aluminum foil to save yourself a time-consuming cleanup job. Prevent other messes by using parchment paper, oven bags or roasting pans with lids.

SALT A GREASE SPILL WHILE COOKING

If grease spills over in your oven while you're roasting meat, sprinkle salt over the grease before it has a chance to bake on. Close the oven door and let the cooking continue. By cleanup time, the spill will have transformed itself into an easily removable pile of ash.

Take Care Even though it may be tempting, don't use abrasive cleaning products on your oven and definitely not a wire brush. You may damage the enamel surface.

Keep a Clean Oven

Try these quick and easy ways to keep your oven sparkling clean.

While the oven is still hot, put a heatproof container of hot water inside; the moisture will make it easier to wipe clean.

Place foil or a baking tray underneath a baking or roasting pan—it will save you some elbow grease if the pan's contents boil over.

If your oven is not self-cleaning, while it's still warm, remove burned-on foods with salt and wipe the surface dry with a piece of newspaper or a paper towel. Use a damp cloth to soften any particles that remain so that they can be scrubbed away easily.

Scrub burned-on sugar with newspaper and salt, then wash with soap and water.

The best solution for a thick, crusty buildup on your oven's bottom is salt. Cover bottom with a ½-in.-thick (1.25 cm) layer of coarse rock salt, turn the oven to 200°F and leave it to work for half an hour. Allow oven to cool, vacuum up the salt, then wipe over the oven with a damp cloth.

Baking soda is good for cleaning ovens, too. Heat the oven to 150°F (or the lowest setting), dampen several pieces of paper towel with lukewarm water and sprinkle them with a thick layer of baking soda. Place the pieces of towel on the bottom and sides of the oven (they will stay in place because they're damp). Use a spray bottle to re-moisten the paper towels if they dry out. Once the layer of greasy buildup has softened, remove the paper towels and wipe out the oven with a damp cloth.

You can also try the same salt and baking soda techniques on your baking pans and sheets to remove baked-on residue.

REMOVE OVEN RESIDUE

They may call it a self-cleaning oven, but when it's finished cleaning, you always have to contend with mopping off that ashlike residue. Don't waste a roll of paper towels on the flaky stuff. Clean it up with a few sheets of moistened, crumpled newspaper.

PREVENT GREASE SPLATTERS

How many times have you been burned by splattering grease while cooking bacon when all you wanted was a hearty breakfast? Next time, add a few dashes of salt to the pan before beginning to fry foods that can splatter. You'll cook without pain and you won't have to clean grease off your cooktop.

Stovetop Cleaning SOS!

Need a quick fix? Here's how to keep your stovetop clean and safe to use.

Wipe up splashes and spills on your stovetop immediately—it will save you a lot of extra work.

If food is burned onto an electric heating element, dampen a cloth with soapy water, place on the cold element for 2 hours and wipe it clean. Deal with spills in the grooves of the heating element by slightly heating the element and sprinkling it with a little baking soda, then rubbing it in with a sponge. Wipe it off with a damp sponge or cloth.

Ceramic glass cooktops are especially easy to clean: Simply wipe them with a damp sponge. If food is burned on, sprinkle a little lemon juice on it, let it sit for a few minutes, wipe and, if necessary, remove any residue with a glass scraper. To maintain an attractive shine, polish the cooktop with a little vinegar. And to avoid scratches, lift rather than slide pots and pans from one burner to the next.

MICROWAVE

RECIPE: MICROWAVE OVEN CLEANER

For the price of a lemon, some baking soda or some white vinegar, you can just wipe away the splatters and stains inside your microwave.

- 1½ cups (375 ml) water or 2 cups (500 ml) white vinegar
- 3 Tbsp. lemon juice or 3 Tbsp. baking soda (if using water)

In a microwave-safe bowl, place water or vinegar. If using water, mix in lemon juice or baking soda; if using vinegar, leave plain. Place the uncovered bowl inside the oven, and run the microwave on high for 3 to 5 minutes, allowing the liquid to condense on its inside walls and ceiling.

Carefully remove the bowl with a towel or potholder (it will be very hot!), and wipe the interior of the oven with a dishcloth or paper towel.

USE A LEMON SLICE

Before cleaning your microwave, add a slice of lemon to a bowl of water and heat until steam forms. Then simply wipe out the appliance with a cloth.

MAKE A MINI STEAM BATH

If you don't happen to have a lemon, baking soda or vinegar around, the easiest way to melt the nasty gunk that accumulates on the walls of a microwave is to fill a heatproof glass bowl with water, nuke on high for 2 minutes, keep the door closed for another 2 minutes, and then wipe with a soft rag. The steam will have reconstituted the icky, caked-on muck, making it a cinch to wipe off.

CARPET A DIRTY MICROWAVE FLOOR WITH BAKING SODA

To remove cooked-on spills from the floor or turntable of a microwave, make a paste of 2 parts baking soda to 1 part water and apply it to the hardened goop. After 5 to 6 minutes, wipe up the baking soda with a wet sponge or cloth and remove any residue with a paper towel.

SWEETEN A MICROWAVE

You wiped it down and washed the glass turntable, and yet your microwave still smells like all the dinners you've ever reheated? Vanilla is the answer. Pour a couple of tablespoons (about 30 ml) vanilla into a glass bowl and microwave it on high for 1 minute. Let the vanilla in the bowl cool, then repeat. It will smell as sweet as freshly baked cookies.

REFRIGERATOR

WHEN IN DOUBT—USE VINEGAR

Did you know that vinegar might be an even more effective, safer cleanser for your refrigerator than baking soda? Use equal parts white vinegar and water to wash both the interior and exterior of your fridge, including the door gasket and the fronts of the fruit and vegetable crispers. To prevent mildew growth, wash the inside walls and crisper interiors with full-strength vinegar on a cloth. Also use undiluted vinegar to wipe off accumulated dust and grime on top of your refrigerator. And don't forget to put that box of baking soda inside to keep it smelling clean when you're done.

SCRUB WITH SALT

Another method to keep your refrigerator clean, after you've removed all the food and the racks from the fridge, is to mix a handful of salt into about a gallon (4 L) of warm water and use it with a sponge to clean the inside of the fridge. The mixture isn't abrasive, so it won't scratch surfaces. And you won't be introducing chemical fumes or odors.

Take Care Sticky, syrupy residues can drip down the fridge door and cause it to stick, which may damage the seal. Prevent this potential repair bill by wiping the fridge seal down regularly with a sponge and warm water only. Be careful not to use dishwashing liquid or other detergent, as they may damage the seal.

Uh-Oh, Got Unpleasant Refrigerator Odors?

There are many ways to approach a smelly fridge. Try the one that best suits you and your sniffer.

Avoid stomach-churning odors in the refrigerator by always wrapping foods separately and making sure that containers are tightly covered. If a bad smell does seep through, try placing a bowl of vinegar, half an apple or a little baking soda in an open bag or on a plate or bowl in the fridge.

An open box of baking soda in the refrigerator is the time-honored way to keep odors down, but did you know that tea bags do an even better job? Put three or four tea bags around the fridge, and odors will be readily absorbed. Change them every few weeks for best results.

A food that will absorb food odors? Indeed! To diminish refrigerator smells, peel a raw potato, cut it in half and place each half on a small saucer.

Now place the potato halves on different shelves in the fridge. When the cut surface of a potato turns black, trim the black part away and return the potato to the fridge with its absorbent powers restored.

Sometimes the refrigerator just doesn't smell fresh. Dampen a cotton ball with vanilla extract and place it on a shelf near the back of the fridge. You'll find it acts as a deodorizer, offering its own pleasant scent.

You can also remove refrigerator odors with ease by dabbing a cotton ball or sponge in lemon juice and leaving it in the fridge for several hours. And make sure you toss out any items that might be causing the bad smell.

cont. on p. 28

cont. from p. 27

If a power failure causes the food in your fridge to spoil and become malodorous, you can get rid of those smells in your refrigerator and freezer with the help of some tomato juice. Dispose of the offending food and thoroughly wipe inside the fridge and freezer with a sponge or washcloth doused in undiluted tomato juice. Rinse with warm, soapy water and wipe dry. If traces of smell remain, repeat the procedure or substitute vinegar for the tomato juice.

If something soured in your fridge or if the freezer failed, clean it out, then fill a wide, shallow bowl with fresh coffee grounds and leave it in the fridge or freezer overnight. The strong scent of coffee will permeate the space, eradicating any hint of what went wrong.

Mold and mildew can grab on to your refrigerator and not let go—and banishing the odors takes drastic action. Squeeze a lemon into a cup of water and throw the peel in with the mixture. Unplug the fridge and empty it (we said it was drastic!), nestling ice cream and other meltable items in a tub, sink or ice chest filled with ice. Then, microwave the lemon water to almost boiling and place it inside the empty refrigerator. Close the door and let the deodorizer sit for half an hour. The citrus fumes will freshen the smell and soften any food accumulations. Remove the bowl, wash the fridge's interior, and restock it with your food and beverages.

REFRESH YOUR ICE CUBE TRAYS

If your plastic ice cube trays are covered with hard-water stains—or if it's been a while since you've cleaned them—a few cups (500 ml or so) of white vinegar can help. To remove the spots and cleanse your trays, let them soak in undiluted vinegar for 4 to 5 hours, then rinse well under cold water and allow to dry.

FREEZER CARE

To prevent rapid ice buildup, wipe down the inner freezer walls after you defrost with cooking oil or glycerin. When you defrost next time, the ice will come away from the walls easily.

CLEANING AROUND THE KITCHEN

KEEP WORK SURFACES CLEAN

Kitchen counters and sinks are the perfect spots for germs to breed. From food scraps to potato peels, or the liquid from defrosting a chicken—it all lands on the countertop or sink, harboring countless micro-organisms that can end up on our food. This is why it's absolutely essential to keep these areas meticulously clean. Even when a countertop has been thoroughly cleaned and looks immaculate, there will still be around 1,700 germs per square inch on the surface. But this doesn't mean you have to sterilize your kitchen. Cleaning your counters and sink with hot water and ordinary dishwashing liquid is sufficient. A vinegar solution is another option for cleaning most non-stone countertops.

Take Care

Use vinegar with an acid content of about 6%, not vinegar concentrate, which also is sometimes used for cleaning and may be near other vinegars in the store. No matter what vinegar you clean with, use with care, as the vapors can irritate the eyes and respiratory tract.

REMOVE SPATTERS FROM WALLS

Even the most careful cook cannot avoid an occasional spatter. A busy kitchen takes some wear and tear, but here's a handy remedy for that unsightly grease spot. Sprinkle cornstarch on a soft cloth, then rub the grease spot gently until it disappears.

Vinegar: Go-To Grease Cutter

Every professional cook knows that distilled vinegar is one of the best grease cutters around. It works even on seriously greasy surfaces such as the fry vats used in many food outlets. But you don't need to have a deep fryer to find plenty of ways to put vinegar to good use:

When you've finished frying, clean up grease splatters from stovetop, walls, range hood and non-stone countertops by washing them with a sponge dipped in undiluted white vinegar. Use another sponge soaked in cold tap water to rinse, and wipe dry with a soft cloth.

Pour 3 to 4 tablespoons (45 to 60 ml) white vinegar into your dishwashing liquid and give it a few shakes. The vinegar will increase the detergent's grease-fighting capabilities. You'll need less detergent and save money.

Boiling 2 cups (500 ml) vinegar in a non-cast-iron frying pan for 10 minutes will help keep food from sticking to it for several months at a time.

Remove burned-on grease and food stains from stainless steel cookware by mixing 1 cup (250 ml) distilled vinegar in enough water to cover the stains. (If they're near the top of a large pot, you may need to increase the vinegar.) Let it boil for 5 minutes. Follow with mild scrubbing.

Get that blackened, cooked-on grease off your broiler pan by softening it with a solution of 1 cup (250 ml) apple cider vinegar and 2 tablespoons (30 ml) sugar. Apply the mixture while the tray is still hot, and let it sit for an hour or so. Give it a light scrubbing and watch the grime slide off easily.

Got a hot plate that looks more like a grease pan? Whip it back into shape by washing it with a sponge dipped in full-strength white vinegar.

GIVE GREASE STAINS THE SLIP

Eliminate grease stains from your kitchen table or non-stone countertops by wiping them down with a cloth dampened in a solution of equal parts white vinegar and water. In addition to removing the grease, the vinegar will neutralize any odors on the surface (once its own pungent aroma has evaporated, that is).

ERASE PERMANENT MARKERS

If you have the unhappy task of removing permanent marker from a countertop, don't worry; most countertops are made of nonpermeable material such as plastic laminate or granite. Rubbing alcohol will dissolve the marker into a liquid so you can wipe it right off.

Surface Care

Countertops and other well-used surfaces in your kitchen require daily attention to keep them clean and free of mold and bacteria.

Laminate or granite surfaces can be washed off with a sponge and a soap solution, or even with 1 part vinegar and 1 part water. (Natural stone such as granite is acid sensitive, so research before using vinegar on stone.) Quickly wipe dry to avoid streaks.

Wipe down large surfaces with a cloth in each hand: one for cleaning, the other for drying.

To reduce germs from work surfaces, scrub unsealed wood surfaces regularly with salt or a mixture of 4 tablespoons (60 ml) baking soda and 2 tablespoons (30 ml) lemon juice.

To make wood surfaces dirt resistant, rub them with a little olive oil or linseed oil after cleaning and removing water stains.

When cleaning cabinets, inside or out, add a little vinegar to the soapy water to cut through grease.

A JOB FOR WASHING SODA

Washing soda (a common name for sodium carbonate) is good for tackling greasy messes. Dissolve a cup of washing soda in a quart of hot water and add a dash of all-purpose cleaner. You can use this solution on dirty dishes (such as soaking greasy pans), but it is also good for removing mold and as a drain cleaner. Wear rubber gloves when handling washing soda and take care to avoid contact with the eyes.

ALL-PURPOSE CLEANER

For glass, stainless steel and plastic laminate surfaces, fill a repurposed spray bottle with 2 parts water, 1 part distilled white vinegar and a couple of drops of dishwashing liquid.

ALMOST-FREE ALL-PURPOSE CLEANER

Why buy an antibacterial spray cleaner if you can make one in less than 5 minutes? In a repurposed spray bottle, combine 1 cup (250 ml) rubbing alcohol, 1 cup (250 ml) water and 1 tablespoon (15 ml) white vinegar. Spritz onto kitchen surfaces including tile and chrome, then wipe off.

WHITE GOODS CLEANER

Regular wiping with this solution will remove grubby finger marks and leave the surfaces of freezers, refrigerators and washing machines looking like new without a scratch.

8	tsp. (40 ml) dishwashing liquid
1	oz. (28 g) cornstarch
1	cup (250 ml) water
1	cup (250 ml) white vinegar
	Few drops of herbal essential oil

Put all the ingredients in a repurposed spray bottle and shake gently to combine.

Spray a fine mist of the mixture over the grubby surface and wipe clean with a soft cloth.

LEMON STAIN LIFTER

Getting that tomato sauce stain out is easier than you think. Simply wet the stain with lemon juice, let it sit for 30 minutes or so, and then sprinkle baking soda on the abrasive side of an all-purpose kitchen sponge and scrub the discolored area. Most stains will vanish, and your kitchen will smell fresher.

CABINET TOPS

Greasy dirt on the tops of kitchen cabinets tends to build up in an especially thick layer. Easy prevention: Run sheets of old newspaper on the tops of kitchen cabinets and stick it down with adhesive tape so that it can't be seen from below (note that paper toweling won't work as well as newspapers). Simply change the paper as needed and save yourself a lot of scrubbing.

Handy Hack

Rub a little cooking oil into the rubber seals of kitchen appliances occasionally so they will close tightly.

REPLACE PAPER TOWELS WITH CLEAN RAGS

One way to go green in the kitchen with ease is to quit buying, using and discarding paper towels. Cut up absorbent cotton, such as a T-shirt knit, into small squares and use them, unhemmed, for quick kitchen cleanups like spilled juice. Then throw these used kitchen rags into the wash. Save paper towels only for the greasiest cleanups, such as draining cooked bacon.

CLUB SODA CLEANSE

Pour club soda directly on stainless steel countertops, ranges and sinks, wipe with

SCOURING POWDER

You don't need chlorine bleach to clean stains off the nonporous surfaces in your kitchen and bathroom. This scouring powder is very effective, a lot safer to use and far more economical.

- 1   cup (250 ml) baking soda
- 1   cup (250 ml) borax
- 1   cup (250 ml) salt
- 1   clean 32-oz. (1 L) container with cover

Combine the ingredients in the container and mix well. Close the container tightly to store.

To clean a stained surface, sprinkle some of the powder onto a damp sponge or directly onto the surface to be cleaned. Scour, rinse and dry.

a soft cloth, rinse with warm water, and wipe dry. To clean porcelain fixtures, simply pour club soda over them and wipe with a soft cloth. There's no need for soap or rinsing, and the soda will not mar the finish. You can also give the inside of your fridge a good cleaning with

Baking Soda to the Rescue

Try these 10 nonbaking uses for baking soda.

1. Remove stains from plastic utensils and rubber spatulas with a baking soda paste rubbed on with a sponge or scouring pad.

2. Protect stained enamel cookware, which can be scratched by abrasive cleaners, by coating the stain with a baking soda paste—then wipe it off after an hour.

3. Add 2 tablespoons (30 ml) baking soda to your dishwashing liquid to clean greasy dishes.

4. Deodorize your dishwasher by pouring in half a box of baking soda and running the empty washer through the rinse cycle.

5. Dip a damp cloth in baking soda and rub it on china to remove coffee stains.

6. Shine stainless steel by sprinkling it with baking soda and rubbing with a damp cloth.

7. Moisten grease stains on your stovetop with water, cover with baking soda and wipe.

8. Clean your coffee maker by brewing 1 quart (1 L) water mixed with ¼ cup (60 ml) baking soda.

9. Loosen burned-on food from cast-iron skillets by adding 2 tablespoons (30 ml) baking soda to 1 quart (1 L) water and boiling solution for 5 minutes.

10. Remove thermos residue with ¼ cup (60 ml) baking soda and 1 quart (1 L) water. Soak overnight.

a weak solution of club soda and a little bit of salt.

REMOVE RUST FROM KNIVES

Forget about using steel wool or harsh chemicals—how's this for an easy way to get the rust off your kitchen or utility knives? Plunge your rusty knife into a large onion three or four times (if it's very rusty, it may require a few extra stabs). The only tears you shed will be ones of joy over your rust-free blade.

WHITEN BONE HANDLES

In time, bone-handled knives begin to yellow. Unless you love the antiqued look, wrap a yellowed handle in a piece of flannel moistened with hydrogen peroxide. Let it sit for a day or so, then unwrap. Rinse and dry the knife, and the handle will be good as new.

TOASTER VS. BRUSH

If your toaster is clogged with hard-to-reach crumbs, unplug it and loosen the crumbs with a small paintbrush or soft toothbrush. Avoid damaging the machine's heating elements by brushing very lightly. Once you've broken the stubborn crumbs apart, turn the toaster upside down, hold it over the kitchen sink and gently shake out the debris.

Insider Tip Dip an old toothbrush into soapy water and use it to clean between appliance knobs and buttons, and all around raised-letter nameplates.

DIY CABINET POLISH

Why burn through your household budget on furniture polish for those large wood kitchen cabinets, bookshelves or wardrobes around your home? This is the perfect polish to use on big jobs—and it costs almost nothing to make. Be sure to mix up a fresh batch for each use.

1   tsp. (5 ml) lemon juice
1   tsp. (5 ml) olive oil
2   cups (500 ml) warm water

Combine the ingredients in a bowl or container.

Dip a soft flannel cloth into the solution and wring it out. Wipe over the wood.

Buff and polish with a soft, dry cloth.

BRUSH CAN OPENER BLADES

Does that dirty wheel blade of your electric can opener look as if it's seen at least one can too many? To clean it, dip an old toothbrush in white vinegar and position the bristles of the brush around the side and edge of the wheel. Turn on the appliance and let the blade scrub itself clean.

KEEP APPLIANCES DUST-FREE

Sometimes it seems that dust gathers more quickly on countertop appliances than anywhere. If this happens to you, cover the appliances with dish towels or—if you're always looking for still one more way to use pantyhose—a stocking leg cut to size.

EASY BLENDER CLEANING

Sure, you always flush out the blender jar under the kitchen sink faucet, and sometimes you even give it a proper washing. But that's hardly enough to keep it hygienically correct. Pour 1 cup (250 ml) water and ¼ cup (60 ml) vinegar into the jar and add a squirt of dishwashing liquid. Put on the jar top and blend the mixture for 1 minute. Now rinse the jar and wipe it dry, and your blender will be ready to whir.

MAKE BRASS AND COPPER POLISH

When exposure to the elements dulls brass or copper items, there's no need to buy expensive cleaning products. To shine your candlesticks or remove green tarnish from copper pots, make a paste by mixing equal parts salt, flour and vinegar. Use a soft cloth to rub this over the item, rinse with warm, soapy water, and buff back to its original shine.

RESTORE A SPONGE

Hand sponges and mop sponges usually get grungy beyond use long before they are really worn out. To restore sponges to a pristine state, soak them overnight in a solution of about ¼ cup (60 ml) salt per quart (1 L) water.

PICK UP SPILLED EGGS

If you've ever dropped an uncooked egg, you know what a mess it is to clean up.

Cover the spill with salt. It will draw the egg together and you can easily wipe it up with a sponge or paper towel.

Insider Tip Use undiluted white vinegar on your hands to remove stains from berries and other fruits.

REMOVE STAINS ON HANDS

Your family's favorite carrot soup is simmering on the stove, and you have the orange hands to show for it. Hard-to-remove stains on hands from peeling carrots or handling pumpkin come right off if you rub your hands with a cut raw potato.

TAKE DOWN WAXY BUILDUP

Use club soda for wax buildup on vinyl. Working in sections, pour a little club soda onto a vinyl floor and scrub it with the abrasive side of a kitchen sponge. Let the soda sit for 5 minutes, then wipe up the loosened wax with a wad of cheesecloth or pantyhose.

REMOVE ODORS

PANTRY DEODORIZER

Vinegar is a valuable basic to have in your pantry. An open bowl of vinegar effectively fights unpleasant odors as it evaporates. And don't worry, the vinegar smell vanishes quickly after airing.

LINGERING SMELL ON HANDS

There is nothing more irritating than a strong fish, onion or garlic smell that sticks to your hands. Here's the cheap and easy answer. Wash your hands with soap and water as usual, then pour vinegar over your clean hands and rub in for a few seconds. Rinse and dry hands as usual.

You'll find that these scents are a lot easier to wash off if you rub some distilled vinegar on your hands before and after you slice vegetables or clean fish.

SOMETHING'S FISHY

Before preparing fresh fish, halve a lemon and rub both hands with the cut ends to help keep them from absorbing odors. (If you didn't know you had a tiny scratch or cut on your hand, you will now!) If you fried the fish in a non-cast-iron pan, wash the pan and pour in ½ inch (1.25 cm) white vinegar; the acetic acid should banish any lingering fish smell.

absorb most of the unpleasant odors. For cauliflower, try half a lemon.

BAKE AN AIR FRESHENER

Don't buy an air freshener when you can get rid of kitchen odors at a fraction of the cost with baked lemon. Simply slice two lemons, put them on a foil-lined cookie sheet and bake in a preheated oven at 225°F for 60 to 90 minutes. To prolong the cleansing effect once the heat's turned off, open the oven door and let the slices sit for a few hours.

CLEAR THE AIR OF GREASE

An old southern trick to prevent a kitchen smelling of grease while chicken is frying is to put a small dish of white vinegar in the kitchen. The grease will miraculously collect on the surface rather than hanging in the air. Try it and see.

FREEZE IT OUT!

Got a musty-smelling book or a plastic container with a fish odor? Place them in the freezer overnight. By morning they'll be fresh again. It works with almost any other small item that has a bad smell you want to be rid of.

Insider Tip Cinnamon, anyone? Mask odors by boiling water with a little cinnamon in a small pot while cooking.

ABSORB VEGETABLE ODORS

Love broccoli, but hate the smell while it's cooking? Try putting a piece of white bread on top of the pot when cooking up a batch of "smelly" vegetables. It will

GET RID OF SMOKE ODOR

If you've burned a steak or something else, remove the lingering smoky odor by placing a shallow bowl about three-fourths full of white or cider vinegar in the room where the scent is strongest. Use several bowls if the smell permeates your entire home. You can also quickly dispense of the smell of fresh cigarette smoke in a room by moistening a cloth with vinegar and waving it around a bit.

GARBAGE CAN TIPS

BAKING SODA DOES THE TRICK

If something smells "off" in your kitchen, it's probably emanating from your garbage can. Some smells linger even after you dispose of the offending garbage, so be sure to give your kitchen garbage can a cleaning with a wet paper towel dipped in baking soda (wear an old pair of rubber gloves for this job). Rinse the can out with a damp sponge and let it dry before inserting a new bag. You can also ward off bad smells by sprinkling a bit of baking soda into the bottom of the can before inserting the bag.

A BIT OF CITRUS

Empty the kitchen garbage can frequently and, if possible, compost all fruit and vegetable peelings (but not meat or cooked foods, as these can attract vermin). If bad odors do develop, add orange or lemon peel to the can.

BORAX IN THE BIN

Garbage cans are great incubators for odor-causing mold and bacteria. To fend off accumulations of these microscopic marauders, sprinkle ½ cup (125 ml) borax in the bottom of your garbage can and renew it with every emptying.

TRY A DEEPER CLEAN

Let's be real: Our garbage cans stink. The smell doesn't have to linger, though. You can use hydrogen peroxide to clean the can and get rid of foul odors. Pour 3% hydrogen peroxide in the bottom of the can and let it sit overnight. The next day, pour water into the can, swish it around and dump the excess mixture. You can also spray hydrogen peroxide along the inside of the can and rinse it out to get an even deeper clean. Your nose will thank you later.

CUTTING BOARDS

OIL IT UP

Brush your wooden cutting board with cooking oil every few weeks. You'll reduce the board's tendency to absorb moisture and limit microbe growth.

Take Care Don't place a wet wooden cutting board on a heater to dry as this will cause cracks to appear in the surface.

HOW TO CLEAN WOOD

To clean your wooden cutting boards or a butcher block countertop, wipe them with full strength white vinegar after each use. The acetic acid in the vinegar is effective against such harmful bugs as E. coli, salmonella and staphylococcus. Never use water and dishwashing liquid on wood; it can weaken surface wood fibers. When wooden cutting surfaces also need deodorizing, spread some baking soda over them and spray on undiluted white vinegar. Let it foam and bubble for 5 to 10 minutes, then rinse with a cloth dipped in clean, cold water.

STAINS ON BOARD

Orange stains left on a non-wood cutting board after cutting carrots can be almost impossible to remove by washing in water. As the pigment in carrots is fat soluble, an effective approach is smearing the board with vegetable oil before washing. Leave it for a while and then wash with warm soapy water.

FRESHEN CUTTING BOARDS

No wonder your kitchen cutting board smells! After all, you use it to chop onions, crush garlic, cut raw and cooked meat and chicken, and prepare fish. To get rid of the smell and help clean it, rub it all over with the cut side of half a lemon or wash it in undiluted lemon juice straight from the bottle. Lemon will work wonders for your hands as well.

SILVERWARE

DESPOTTING STAINLESS

If you think that vinegar and a paper towel are all you need to rub spots off stainless steel knives, forks and spoons, guess again! The spots will come clean only if you dip the vinegar-soaked paper towel into a saucer of baking soda. After rubbing off the spots, wash the utensils and dry them thoroughly right away.

BRING BACK THE SHINE

For really dirty silverware, use a silver-cleaning cloth. Or leave the items overnight in warm water with a dash of dishwashing liquid added. If the

silver is so tarnished it's black, dissolve a teaspoon (5 ml) of baking soda in a bucket of warm water and place a sheet of aluminum foil in the bottom of the bucket. Place the silver item in the bucket in contact with the foil. Leave for several hours, and the silver becomes shiny again thanks to an electrochemical process that reverses the oxidation. When using this technique, know that it will also restore the shine to any deliberately darkened decorative features (such as on antiqued silver pieces), causing them to disappear.

KETCHUP CAN WORK WONDERS

Some people like a tiny bit of tarnish left in a complex silver pattern to throw the detail into relief, but if you want your silver to shine, shine, shine without rubbing and wearing off the pattern, then ketchup is the way to go. The acids in ketchup will quickly remove every last speck of tarnish from an elaborate silver pattern, leaving it gleaming. Smear a few pieces at a time with ketchup and let them sit for several minutes. Rinse a piece to see how it's coming along. If needed, apply more ketchup, but keep checking so you don't do any damage with the acid. When the silver shines to your satisfaction, rinse with warm water and buff with a soft, lint-free cloth.

MAKE A GENTLE SILVER CLEANER

Don't want to put harsh chemicals on Granny's old silver? Make a cleanser that's less harsh than commercial polishes—and one that won't remove all the tarnish from a complicated pattern, a look many silver lovers prefer because it throws a beautiful pattern into stunning relief. Mix cornstarch with water to make a thick paste. Rub it on the silver and let it dry. Buff off with a lint-free cloth to bring up the shine.

KEEP SILVER FROM TARNISHING

You love serving friends with your fine silver, but polishing it before each use is another story. Put one or two pieces of chalk in the drawer with your good silver; it will absorb moisture and slow tarnishing. Put some in your jewelry box to delay tarnishing there, too.

Handy Hack Remove stuck-on residue from knives with a dishwashing brush or a cork dipped in salt.

FOOD PREP

REMOVE GERMS FROM VEGGIES

You can't be too careful when it comes to food handling and preparation. If you suspect that vegetables have been contaminated or passed through unclean hands, place them in white vinegar for half an hour.

BRUSH BEFORE YOU EAT

Clean craggy vegetables with a soft toothbrush before you cook them.

Brush mushrooms, asparagus and peppers before throwing them into a pot. You'll get rid of dirt that won't normally just wash off the vegetables.

SILK ON YOUR EARS (OF CORN)

Picking individual strands of silk from husked ears of corn is as time-consuming as it is annoying. Get your time and your pleasing temperament back. Dampen a paper towel and rub it gently across the corn. The paper towel will quickly and calmly pick up the silk.

DRY LETTUCE

Making a big salad for a large picnic? Nobody has time to wash and dry six heads of lettuce in a salad spinner—unless you have a really big spinner. Fill the sink with cold water, break up the lettuce heads and wash all the leaves. Lift them into a clean cotton pillowcase, then take it out into the backyard and spin your arm like a propeller. The water will fly in a big circle, and the pillowcase will get wet, but the lettuce leaves will be dry as a bone. Seriously, don't do this indoors.

EAT NAKED FRUIT!

Give your produce a baking soda bath. Dampen fruits (or vegetables) with water, sprinkle a vegetable brush with baking soda and then scrub before you eat them. Rinse well and dry. A baking soda wash removes wax from fruits like apples and reduces pesticides on fruits and veggies that a simple water rinse may not.

CLEAN FISH MORE EASILY

Catching fish is half the battle. Cleaning is the rest! Sprinkle salt liberally on a fish before you start to descale it. You'll find that the scales flick off faster, making the whole job easier.

SOAK OUT FISH SMELLS

Get rid of that fishy smell from store-bought fish fillets and fish steaks by soaking the raw fish for about an hour (inside your refrigerator) in 4 cups (1 L) water with 2 tablespoons (30 ml) baking soda. Rinse the fish well and pat dry before cooking.

CONTAIN A MESSY PROJECT

Cleaning a catch of crabs, peeling shrimp or perhaps coring heaps of apples? Cut open a large paper bag and cover your work surface. When you're done, you can gather together the whole messy pile, paper and all, to discard (or toss onto the compost pile).

IN THE BATHROOM

GENERAL CLEANING

DIY BATHROOM CITRUS CLEANSER

This fragrant cleanser is also kind to the environment.

2	tsp. (10 ml) dishwashing liquid
5	drops lemon oil
1	cup (250 ml) water
5	tsp. (25 ml) citric acid

Mix together the dishwashing liquid and lemon oil. Next, mix the water and citric acid to produce a clear fluid. Add the lemon oil solution to the clear fluid and store in a bottle for up to 3 months.

PLUGGED FAUCET SOLUTION

If a faucet is jammed shut, try pouring club soda over it. It contains small quantities of carbonic acid that help loosen up rust and other forms of corrosion. Leave it for 10 minutes, then gently tap the handle of the faucet with a rubber mallet to get it moving again.

POLISH UP THAT CHROME

Get rid of mineral deposits and polish chrome faucets and other tarnished chrome by simply rubbing lemon rind over the chrome and watching it shine. Rinse well, and dry with a soft cloth.

Take Care
Don't use concentrated vinegar to remove scale from chrome hardware as it will damage the thin layer of chrome plating and attack the brass underneath.

RUBBING ALCOHOL DOES WONDERS

Just reach into the medicine cabinet the next time you need to clean chrome bathroom fixtures. Pour some rubbing alcohol straight from the bottle onto a soft, absorbent cloth and the fixtures. No need to rinse—the alcohol just evaporates. It does a great job of making chrome sparkle, plus it will kill any germs in its path.

REMOVE HARD-WATER BUILDUP

Cut a fresh lemon in half. Then press the lemon onto the end of the faucet. Put a small plastic bag around the lemon and

Clever Natural Bathroom Hacks

Keeping a bathroom clean is essential, but you don't need chemical products to do it. Try these traditional cleaners and cleaning methods to keep your sinks, tiles and fixtures spotless.

Wipe fiberglass bathtubs with a damp cloth and a little bit of baking soda.

Acrylic bathtubs, which are more delicate than steel tubs, have a reputation for being hard to clean. But as long as you shine them up regularly, all you should need is a little dishwashing liquid and water.

Help keep shower areas crystal clear with a soft cloth and a solution of dishwashing liquid and water. Minor soap scum buildup can be rubbed off with vinegar, while serious buildup should be treated with a paste of salt and vinegar applied in a circular motion with a bathtub cleaning brush. Rinse and dry when you're finished. Use a squeegee daily to prevent spots, and rub off any chalky streaks with vinegar.

If mold appears in the shower or bathtub, treat it with vinegar, lemon juice or baking soda.

Remove rust spots by rubbing them with a mixture of water and vinegar.

Whiten grout by scrubbing it with a little toothpaste on an old soft-bristled toothbrush.

Use very fine sandpaper to rub severely discolored grout. Be very careful not to damage the glaze on the tiles.

secure it around the faucet with a rubber band. Be sure that the rubber band is cinched tightly and that the lemon is around the end of the faucet. Leave the lemon in place for a few hours to allow the citric acid to work its magic. After you remove the lemon, you may need to use a gentle scrubbing pad to wash off any loosened hard-water buildup. Then wipe the faucet with a damp cloth to remove any leftover lemon juice. Your faucet will be squeaky clean—and you didn't need to use harsh chemicals!

LEMON LOVE

You can also use a cut lemon to rub accumulated dirt off bathtubs, mirrors and porcelain basins—the acid in the lemon breaks down the mineral scale that accumulates in hard-water areas.

FIGHT MOLD AND MILDEW

To remove and retard bathroom mold and mildew, pour a solution of 3 tablespoons (45 ml) white vinegar, 1 teaspoon (5 ml) borax and 2 cups (500 ml) hot water into a clean repurposed spray bottle and shake well. Spray the mixture on painted surfaces, tiles, windows, wherever you see mold or mildew spots. Use a soft scrub brush on the stains or just let it soak in. Hydrogen peroxide at 3% also works. Don't water it down; just pour it on the offending area and wipe clean. Note that large amounts of mold or mildew, especially on semi-porous surfaces such as flat, painted drywall, may require professional attention.

MULTIPURPOSE CLEANER

Here's a good cleaner that is easy to use and is much cheaper than commercial bathroom cleaners.

2	tsp. (10 ml) borax
½	tsp. (2.5 ml) washing soda
2	Tbsp. (30 ml) lemon juice
¼	cup (60 ml) white vinegar
3	cups (750 ml) very hot water
1	clean 24-oz. (750 ml) repurposed spray bottle

Combine the borax, washing soda, lemon juice and vinegar in the spray bottle.

Slowly add the hot water, then vigorously shake the bottle until the powdered ingredients have dissolved. Shake the bottle before each use.

Spray on tile and ceramic surfaces and wipe with a damp, clean cloth.

Combining vinegar with bleach—or any other product containing chlorine, such as chlorinated lime (sold as bleaching powder)—may produce chlorine gas. In low concentrations, this toxic, acrid-smelling gas can cause damage to your eyes, skin or respiratory system. High concentrations of the gas are often fatal.

QUICK WAYS TO DEODORIZE

Burn matches or light a candle to help curb stale bathroom smells. A potpourri of fragrant herbs and spices—such as cinnamon, rosemary, thyme, cloves or lavender—also does an excellent job.

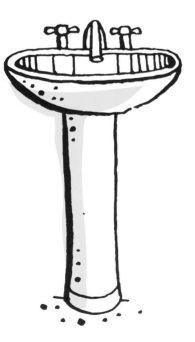

RECIPE: EASY SCRUB

Get out tough stains on surfaces that are easily scratched, including ceramic sinks and countertops.

- ¼ cup (60 ml) borax
- ½ tsp. (2.5 ml) vegetable-oil-based liquid soap, such as castile
- ½ tsp. (2.5 ml) lemon juice

In a small bowl, combine the borax and liquid soap to make a smooth paste.

Stir in the lemon juice; mix well.

Place a small amount on a clean, damp sponge, apply to the surface, then rinse off and dry the surface with a clean cloth.

ODOR ABSORPTION SECRET

Keep your bathroom smelling fresh and clean by placing a decorative dish filled with ½ cup (125 ml) baking soda either on top of the toilet tank or on the floor behind the bowl. You can also make your own bathroom deodorizers by setting out dishes containing equal parts baking soda and your favorite scented bath salts.

Let's Talk Ventilation

Too much moisture creates a breeding ground for mold. Improper ventilation is usually the cause.

If the bathroom or kitchen steams up, air the room at once by opening a window or turning on a fan.

Short, periodic bursts of ventilation are best to maintain air quality. Open windows three times a day for up to 10 minutes in winter, and a little longer in warmer months unless you suffer from hay fever.

Leave about a 1-to-2-inch (2 to 5 cm) clearance between shelves or linen cabinets and outer walls. Mold or mildew can easily develop behind tall furniture.

 Insider Tip In heavy traffic areas such as the bathroom or kitchen, choose a washable wallpaper.

GIVE THE CEILING SOME LOVE

Look up, but prepare yourself for what you might see—spotting, built-up grime and more on a bathroom ceiling. For an easy cleanup, fill a mop bucket with equal parts water and white vinegar. Then don goggles or other protective eyewear. Dip a long-handled sponge mop into the bucket, squeeze it out and reach up to clean one section of ceiling at a time. One more spick-and-span surface.

BRUSH AWAY RUST STAINS

To get rid of hard-water rust stains on commodes, tubs and sinks, just squeeze a little toothpaste onto an old toothbrush and scrub away. Or scrub the stain with a paste of borax and lemon juice. Whichever method you choose, attack rust stains right away. The sooner you deal with them, the easier they are to remove simply.

SCRUB THAT TUB

Let this simple solution of cream of tartar and hydrogen peroxide do the hard work of removing a bathtub stain for you. Fill a small, shallow cup or dish with cream of tartar and add hydrogen peroxide drop by drop until you have a thick paste. Apply to the stain and let it dry. When you remove the dried paste, you'll find that the stain is gone too.

RECIPE: NONTOXIC RUST REMOVER

Commercial rust removers are among the most toxic compounds found around the home. But here's a completely safe and surprisingly effective way to give rust stains on bathtubs and sinks the brushoff.

1	lime (a second one may be needed for some jobs)
¼	cup (60 ml) salt

Squeeze the lime over the rust spots, then cover the moistened area with salt.

Let the mixture sit 3 to 4 hours.

Use a nylon scrubber to scrub the mixture off. The rust should be gone. Repeat for really

 Take Care Hydrogen peroxide is considered corrosive— even in the relatively weak 3% solution sold as a household antiseptic. Never put it in or anywhere near your eyes or around your nose. And don't ever swallow it or try to set it on fire, either.

MUST-DO'S FOR TUBS AND SINKS

Easily get the gunk off old porcelain bathtubs and sinks by applying a paste of 2 parts baking soda and 1 part hydrogen peroxide. Let the paste sit for about half an hour. Then give it a good scrubbing and rinse well. The paste will also sweeten the drain as it washes down.

Insider Tip In the bathroom, use vinegar to clean the corners between the shower or bath and the tiled wall regularly.

ICKY TOOTHBRUSH HOLDER?

Get the grime, bacteria and caked-on toothpaste drippings out of the grooves of your bathroom toothbrush holder by cleaning the openings with cotton swabs moistened with white vinegar.

WASH OUT THE RINSE CUP

If several people in your home use the same rinse cup after brushing their teeth, give it a weekly cleaning by filling it with equal parts water and white vinegar, or just full-strength vinegar, and let it sit overnight. Rinse thoroughly with cold water before using again.

NAIL CLIPPER CLEANSE

It's important to clean nail clippers, especially since harmful bacteria and fungi could linger on their surfaces. Luckily, hydrogen peroxide can help. Simply pour hydrogen peroxide into a container, submerge the nail clippers for 3 to 5 minutes and then dry them with a paper towel.

SHOWER SHINE

WHITE VINEGAR IS YOUR FRIEND

Keep a repurposed spray bottle filled with vinegar and a sponge by (or in) the shower so you can make washing down the surfaces part of your post-shower routine.

scrub it on the shower doors with a sponge—and, if you have time, all the other shower surfaces as well.

THE SECRET TO SPARKLE

Getting soap film off your glass shower door just got easier. Use dishwashing liquid, and you will be amazed at how quickly and easily the gunk comes off.

GET A SUPER SPARKLE

If you'd rather, for even more of a cleaning punch, make a solution of ¼ cup (60 ml) dishwashing liquid, ¼ cup (60 ml) hydrogen peroxide and ¼ cup (60 ml) baking soda. Then

Shower Curtain Care

The moist environment of a bathroom is just made for mold and mildew, so don't be surprised when it pops up on your shower curtain. You can keep it at bay for a while, at least, by soaking curtains and liners in salt water before hanging them. Once they're up, if any gunk appears, try one of these methods:

Use a paste of washing soda and a little water. Rub on thoroughly, then rinse off. Finish by washing the shower curtain in your washing machine at 90°F. Do not spin!

Add ½ cup (125 ml) borax and ½ cup (125 ml) vinegar to 2 cups (500 ml) water, pour onto the affected areas and let sit for 8 to 10 minutes. Then scrub with a sponge or cloth.

Make a paste of vinegar and salt and spread it on the concerning area. Let it dry 1 to 2 hours and then clean it with a damp cloth.

TRICKY SHOWER DOOR TRACKS

Use vinegar to remove accumulated dirt and grime from the tracks of your shower doors. Fill the tracks with about 2 cups (500 ml) full-strength white vinegar and let it sit for 3 to 5 hours. (If the tracks are really dirty, heat the vinegar in a glass container for 30 seconds in your microwave first.) Then pour some hot water over the track to flush away the gunk. You may need to use a small scrubbing brush, or even an old toothbrush, to get up tough stains.

Take Care

Never use cleaning products that contain solvents on acrylic or plastic shower doors. **Apart from the fact that these products are harmful to the environment and your health, they will leave plastic surfaces dull and sticky as they start to dissolve the material.**

Simple Tips: Descale a Showerhead or Faucet Aerator

For a Showerhead Unscrew the showerhead and soak overnight in a bowl of white vinegar (if it has several parts, unscrew these if possible and soak separately).

Remove any remaining scale or mineral deposits with an old toothbrush. If the showerhead can't be unscrewed, pour the vinegar into a plastic bag and pull it up around the head to immerse it. Secure firmly in place with twist ties or string and leave overnight. Finish off with the toothbrush the following day.

For a Faucet Aerator An aerator is a piece of hardware that screws onto the end of a faucet. It is a fine sieve that introduces air into the water stream to reduce splashing. When mineral deposits are visible even on the outer ring that holds the sieve in place, it's high time to give the aerator a thorough cleaning.

With a thin cloth wrapped around the ring to prevent damage, unscrew aerator with a pair of tongue and groove pliers.

Place the outer ring and the sieve in a bowl of white vinegar and leave for several hours. Then rinse both components thoroughly and screw back onto the faucet.

TILE MAINTENANCE

CREAM OF TARTAR TRICK

Got a bathtub ring that won't scrub off or stubborn stains on the tile? They're no match for hydrogen peroxide and cream of tartar. Put a few tablespoons (30 ml) cream of tartar in a cup or jar, then add hydrogen peroxide by the drop to make a thick paste. (If you accidentally add way too much liquid, you may want to dump half the entire cup before stirring in more cream of tartar—or you may find that your container will be empty fast!) Spread onto the stain and let it dry. Rinse with warm water, and the stain should be history.

SOLUTION FOR STUBBORN SCUM AND WATER SPOTS

Nonporcelain surfaces in the bathroom—including ceramic tiles around sinks and tubs, and fiberglass and acrylic shower stalls—can become dulled by water spots and built-up scum just as easily as tubs and sinks. Tackle these heavily soiled surfaces with vigor and 2 cups (500 ml) salt dissolved in 1 gallon (4 L) hot water. After applying, let it sit about 15 minutes, then scrub off and rinse.

STAIN IN GROUT

Get out a little fine-grit sandpaper to help you remove stains from grout.

GOOD RIDDANCE TO GRIME

The grouting between bathroom tiles is a magnet for dirt and germs, and it's easy to miss these hard-to reach crevices during regular cleaning. Every so often make a paste of 1 part borax, 2 parts baking soda and 1 to 2 parts water and scrub it onto the grout with a toothbrush.

CLEAN GROUT OUT

You can clean heavily soiled grout with a paste made up of washing soda (sodium carbonate) and a little water. Leave for about an hour, then scrub clean with a brush or old toothbrush and rinse well. Use an acidic descaling agent such as citric acid to remove mineral scale, but rinse the grout thoroughly with clean water before and after to prevent damage.

WHITEN IT UP

Has the grout between the tiles of your shower or bathtub enclosure become stained or discolored? Restore it to its original shade of white by using a toothbrush dipped in undiluted white vinegar to scrub away the dinginess.

EUCALYPTUS TILE CLEANER

This fresh, tangy powder will leave your kitchen and bathroom tiles shiny and clean for a fraction of the price of commercial cleaners.

- ½ **cup (125 ml) pure soap flakes (or a bar of pure soap)**
- 1 **cup (250 ml) chalk or diatomaceous earth**
- 1 **cup (250 ml) baking soda**
- 1 **tsp. (5 ml) eucalyptus essential oil**
- 1 **clean repurposed 16-oz. (500 ml) jar with metal top**

If you cannot find soap flakes, lightly grate a bar of pure soap on a coarse kitchen grater. Then, in a small bowl, crush the soap flakes with the back of a spoon until powdered (or grind them in a blender).

Mix in chalk or diatomaceous earth and the baking soda, breaking up any lumps.

Sprinkle the essential oil over the surface of the powdered mixture and stir it with the spoon. Stir for several minutes to disperse oil throughout the mixture, then spoon the mixture into a screw-top jar or can with some holes punched in the lid.

Cover the holes with masking tape to keep the powder dry between uses. Let the mixture sit for 1 week before using to be sure the essential oil has been thoroughly absorbed. Sprinkle surface with powder, scrub with a damp sponge and rinse with clear water. Dry with a soft towel.

DRAIN KNOW-HOW

FAST AND EASY DRAIN FRESHENER

Here's an easy way to eliminate drain odors while maintaining the proper pH and health of your septic system. Run warm tap water for several seconds, then pour 1 cup (250 ml) baking soda into the drain. Wait about an hour and flush with a teapot of boiling water. For best results, repeat once every 2 weeks.

CLEAR CLOGS

Before you reach for a caustic drain cleaner to unclog the bathroom or kitchen drain, try this much gentler approach. Use a funnel to insert ½ cup (125 ml) borax into the drain and slowly pour in 2 cups (500 ml) boiling water. Let the mixture sit for 15 minutes, then flush with hot water. Repeat for stubborn clogs.

Insider Tip

Use a small, flat strainer to prevent hair from going down the drain hole and clogging the drain in the first place.

DIY DRAIN OPENER

Don't bother with those caustic commercial cleaners; try this simple, inexpensive and safe way to unclog drains instead.

- ½   cup (125 ml) baking soda
- 1   cup (250 ml) vinegar
- 1   teapot boiling water

Pack the drain with baking soda, then pour in vinegar.

Keep the drain covered for 10 minutes, then flush it out with boiling water.

GOT SLOW DRAINS?

If you have a slow drain and nothing else in the house on hand to fix it, pour a 32-ounce (1 L) bottle of cola down the drain to remove the clog.

MIRROR, MIRROR

CLEAN WINDOWS AND MIRRORS

To get windows and mirrors spotless and streakless, just wash them with a clean sponge dipped in 2 tablespoons (30 ml) borax dissolved in 3 cups (750 ml) water.

TEA CAN BRING THE SHINE

To make mirrors shine, brew a pot of strong tea, let it cool, then use it to clean the mirrors. Dampen a soft cloth in the tea and wipe it all over the surface of the mirrors. Buff with a soft, dry cloth for a sparkly, streak-free shine.

GET THAT GLEAM

Keep mirrors gleaming with a mixture of warm water and vinegar. Combine 1 cup (250 ml) white vinegar with 1 quart (1 L) warm water and rub on the mirror with a soft cloth.

SAY BYE TO STREAKS

If you want a natural cleaner that will leave your mirror streak-free, look no further than hydrogen peroxide. Simply put 3% hydrogen peroxide in a repurposed spray bottle, spray the mirror and wipe. This simple solution will make your mirrors shine!

Handy Hack

Clean a mirror by rubbing it with a potato cut in half, then rinsing with water and polishing. It will keep bathroom fog at bay, too.

REMOVE STICKY HAIR SPRAY

When you are spritzing your head with hair spray, some of it inevitably winds up on the mirror. A quick wipe with rubbing alcohol will whisk away that sticky residue and leave your mirror looking sparkling clean and shiny again.

THE BEST DE-FOGGING TRICK

Prevent fogging by coating mirrors with shaving cream or toothpaste and wiping them dry with a towel before showering.

TOP TOILET TIPS

START A BAKING SODA ROUTINE

Instead of using chemicals to clean the toilet bowl, just pour half a box of baking soda into the tank once a month. Let it stand overnight, then give it a few flushes in the morning. This actually cleans both the tank and the bowl. You can also pour 2 to 3 tablespoons (30 to 45 ml) baking soda directly into the toilet bowl and scrub any stains. Wait a few minutes, then flush them away.

WHITE VINEGAR FOR THE WIN

An easy way to keep the toilet looking and smelling clean is to pour 2 cups (500 ml) white vinegar into the bowl and let the solution soak overnight before flushing. Including this vinegar soak in your weekly cleaning regimen will also help keep away ugly water rings that typically appear just above water level.

TRY ONE OF THESE HOUSEHOLD ITEMS FOR A FRESH FLUSH

If you prefer not to use toilet bowl cleaner, and you don't have much else around, pour a capful of mouthwash or the contents of a can of cola into the toilet. Leave it for half an hour, scrub with a toilet brush, then flush clean.

TOILET PAPER ANTI-SCALE TECHNIQUE

Remove ugly toilet bowl scale by leaving a layer of toilet paper soaked in vinegar on the mineral deposits overnight and rubbing the deposits off in the morning.

Handy Hack

Avoid unpleasant-looking urine scale by putting just a dash of vinegar in the bottom of the toilet bowl once a week and letting it sit overnight.

Clean a Toilet the Natural Way

See which one of these super-easy-to-make recipes may work best for you.

DIY NONTOXIC TOILET BOWL CLEANER

Clean and sanitize your toilet bowl without harmful chlorine! For no-scrub convenience, simply pour in this mixture and leave overnight.

- 1 **cup (250 ml) borax**
- ½ **cup (125 ml) white vinegar**

Flush the toilet to wet the sides of the bowl.

Sprinkle the borax around the toilet bowl, then liberally drizzle some vinegar on top. Let the toilet sit undisturbed for 3 to 4 hours before scrubbing with a toilet brush.

TOUGHER TOILET CLEANER

For tougher jobs, try this potent paste that still has no chlorine and costs much less than commercial toilet bowl cleaners.

- ⅔ **cup (160 ml) borax**
- ⅓ **cup (80 ml) lemon juice**

In a small bowl, combine the ingredients to form a paste.

Apply the paste to the toilet bowl using a sponge or rag. Let the paste sit for 2 hours, then scrub off. Flush the toilet.

HOMEMADE TABLETS

If you are looking for an alternative to toilet cleaner for a less resilient surface, make your own tablets.

- ½ **cup (125 ml) citric acid**
- 1 **cup (250 ml) bicarbonate of soda**
- 2 **to 3 drops tea tree essential oil**
  Water
  Silicone molds

Mix citric acid with bicarbonate of soda, 2 to 3 drops tea tree essential oil, and a little water.

Press into silicone molds and leave to dry.

DAWN DISHWASHING LIQUID CAN REPLACE A PLUNGER!

If you don't have a plunger handy, here's a trick: Use Dawn dishwashing liquid to unclog a toilet. Squirt a generous amount of soap into the clogged bowl. Wait until the water level goes down, fill a bucket with cool water (hot water could crack the bowl), and then pour it into the soaped toilet from waist high. The clog should clear—though you may need to repeat the procedure a few times. This works only if the clog is paper or organic.

SPICK-AND-SPAN TOILET BRUSH

To clean a toilet brush, mix 3 cups (750 ml) of washing soda in a bucket of cold water. Leave the brush to soak in the mixture for a few hours.

Handy Hack

Add a quick dash of vinegar and water to the bottom of a toilet brush holder to keep it from getting smelly.

SEPTIC TANK ACTIVATOR

If you detect a persistent unpleasant odor from the septic tank, it's probably due to a "die-off" of sewage-digesting bacteria. Before you call in your local septic tank specialist, try using this simple recipe to give the little beasties a boost.

- 2 **cups (500 ml) sugar**
- 4 **cups (1 L) simmering water**
- 2 **cups (500 ml) cornmeal**
- 2 **packages (¼ oz. or 7 g each) dry yeast**

Dissolve the sugar in a saucepan of simmering water and cool to lukewarm. Mix in the cornmeal and the yeast.

Once the solution has been mixed, flush it down the toilet (flush twice, if necessary). For best results, do this before turning in for the night or when there will be no activity in the bathroom for several hours.

IN THE
LAUNDRY

ESSENTIAL LAUNDRY CARE

How To: Save Energy & Money

Get your laundry done beautifully in an environmentally friendly way. It just takes an energy-efficient washing machine—and a few helpful tips.

Avoid the prewash cycle, which is not necessary for most laundry.

Choose the appropriate washing program so that the water level matches the laundry load. This protects the machine, especially during the spin cycle.

Take water hardness into account—the softer the water, the less detergent you need.

Never use more detergent than the manufacturer recommends. You'll get soap overflow.

CLEAN THE MACHINE

A simple way to periodically clean out soap scum in your washing machine is to add 2 cups (500 ml) white vinegar and run the machine through a full cycle without any clothes or detergent. If your machine is particularly dirty, fill it with very hot water, add 2 gallons (7.5 L) vinegar and let the agitator run for 8 to 10 minutes. Turn off the machine and let it stand overnight. The next day, drain it, then run the machine through a complete cycle.

Take Care

Don't wash in cold or warm water all the time. Run your washing machine on a hot water cycle every now and then—otherwise a bacterial film will build up and the machine will start to smell.

WASH TOWELS TOGETHER

Make the most of your washing machine's capacity. Towels get heavy when they are full of water, so washing several at the same time can prevent the machine from getting out of balance. Doing a large load also saves on water and homemade laundry soap.

USE SALT TO SET COLOR—REALLY!

The first two or three times you wash new colored towels, add 1 cup (250 ml) salt to the wash. The salt will set the colors so that your towels remain bright much longer.

IF YOU'VE HAD A SWEATY DAY, WASH YOUR SHIRT RIGHT AWAY

Don't let a sweaty shirt sit in the hamper. And if it shows some yellowing when it comes out of the wash, don't put it in the dryer. Instead, line-dry the shirt—in the sun, if you can.

Take Care Never shake out or beat clothes affected by mold without wearing a particle face mask (available from hardware stores or online), as the mold spores are harmful to your health.

REACH FOR A POT AND BOIL

With time, white cotton and linen tend to turn yellow—hardly the fresh, crisp look for which cotton is famous. Let sodium come to the rescue by mixing ¼ cup (60 ml) salt and ¼ cup (60 ml) baking soda with 1 gallon (4 L) water in a large cooking pot. Add the yellowed items and boil for 1 hour.

RECIPE: LAUNDRY SOAP

This basic laundry soap gets clothes just as clean as commercial cleaners and it costs a lot less.

- ½ cup (125 ml) pure soap flakes (or a bar of pure soap)
- ½ cup (125 ml) baking soda
- ¼ cup (60 ml) washing soda
- ¼ cup (60 ml) borax
- 1 clean 16-oz. (500 ml) container with lid

If you cannot find soap flakes, lightly grate a bar of pure soap on a coarse kitchen grater.

In a large bowl, mix all the ingredients together. Store in a tightly sealed container.

Use about ½ cup (125 ml) of the mixture instead of detergent in each load of laundry.

Dealing with Mold and Mildew

If your closet has a musty smell, or you discover clothes covered with a whitish or greenish coating, you have a mold or mildew issue.

So how do you get mold and mildew? These troublemakers are the result of humidity, which usually develops when you put away clothes or linens in the closet before they are properly dry. Once the closet doors are closed, humidity remains trapped inside, allowing mold and mildew to grow.

Temperature matters. Another cause of moldy and mildewed clothing can be closets that are located in front of a cold external wall. You can get condensation forming at the back of the closet, creating an environment where molds thrive.

If you suspect there is mold in your closet, clear out and inspect all your clothes and linens. Use your sense of smell too—take action even if there is only a musty smell without any visible signs of mold. Air all clothes and linens thoroughly in the sun before washing to remove the musty smell. Meanwhile, thoroughly clean the closet.

If you find mold on your clothes, you need to act quickly, as only small, relatively fresh mold stains are removable. Rub soap or lemon juice into the stains using a soft brush before machine-washing the items at 140°F or hotter, if possible, and allowing them to dry in full sun. The UV light from the sun will kill any remaining mold spores.

A cleaning agent with citric acid as the active ingredient is useful in the fight against mold, as it will eliminate small mold stains and leave a fresh scent. For a bit more strength, you may need a vinegar cleaner. After cleaning, leave the empty closet open to allow it to dry out and air properly for a few days. You can even place a fan inside or just in front of the closet. For large amounts of mold, get professional advice so as not to spread mold around the house.

To remove mold from upholstery and other fabrics, soak a sponge in ½ cup (125 ml) borax dissolved in 2 cups (500 ml) hot water and rub it into the affected areas. Let it soak in for several hours until the stain disappears and rinse well.

To prevent mold stains, air closets and bedrooms regularly, especially when it's dry outside, and occasionally unfold and re-stack all your folded clothes and linens.

SIMPLE TRICK FOR DINGY SOCKS

If it's getting harder to identify the white socks in your sock drawer, here's a simple way to make them so bright you can't miss them. Start by adding 1 cup (250 ml) vinegar to 2 quarts (2 L) tap water in a large pot. Bring the solution to a boil, pour into a bucket and drop in the dingy socks. Let them soak overnight. The next day, wash them as you normally would.

SALVAGE DISCOLORED WHITES

Don't toss those drab and dingy whites just yet: Dissolve 1 teaspoon (5 ml) cream of tartar in cold water in a clean sink and soak the garment for a few hours before washing. (This is also a great way to restore old handkerchiefs.)

SOFTEN HARD-WATER WASHES

Add ¼ cup (60 ml) baking soda to a hot white wash to boost the strength of your usual detergent and get whites bright.

NEW LIFE FOR SOILED WHITES

It's a sad day when a favorite white shirt or blouse just can't be seen in public anymore—yellow stains, a dreary cast and seemingly permanent ring around the collar. But all is not lost. Perk up the garment by working a paste of vinegar and baking soda directly into stained and soiled areas, then hang the treated garment outside in the sun for a couple of hours. If the collar remains soiled, pour a capful of

Blankets, Pillows and Sheets

Air, shake and clean them—regularly! Plus, follow these tips:

Air and shake out bedding regularly. This distributes the filling evenly and combats dust mites and other pests that like warm, dark places.

Add 2 cups (500 ml) white vinegar to your machine's rinse water (or a laundry tub filled with water) to remove soap residue from cotton and wool blankets before drying. This will also leave them feeling fresh and soft as new.

Hang quilts, blankets and pillows outside on a clothesline on a dry day. However, don't hang out anything with a feather filling in intense sunlight, as this is likely to make the feathers brittle and porous.

Use a gentle detergent or hair shampoo to wash feather or down pillows, then put them in the dryer at a low temperature along with a clean tennis ball, which prevents the filling from clumping. Do not vacuum down or feather quilts, or you risk thinning out the filling.

If you suffer from allergies, wash your bedding frequently and use pillows, quilts and blankets made from synthetic materials or rayon and with synthetic filling, not feathers. These are easier to wash and dry to get rid of mites.

Curtain Call!

They need love, too. Cleaning them isn't a chore when you follow this advice.

Soak colored curtains in salt water to prevent fading and to help dissolve dirt.

Wash delicate curtains by hand in the bathtub with plenty of hand soap.

Protect sheer curtains in the washing machine by putting them in a pillowcase.

Always wash curtains using the machine's delicate cycle with plenty of water. That should help to reduce the amount of creasing.

Allow hand-washed curtains to drip dry; never wring them out. To be sure they hang properly, weight the bottom edges with clothespins before hanging them.

To prevent shrinking, stretch out cotton curtains while still wet.

Stiffen sheer curtains with a solution of 1 part sugar and 3 parts water added to the last rinse, or put them in water used for boiling rice.

Machine-washable cotton drapes often come out wrinkled. To keep wrinkling to a minimum, dissolve 1 tablespoon (15 ml) plain gelatin in 1 cup (250 ml) boiling water and add to the final rinse cycle. The same trick restores shine to polished cotton curtains.

Give your curtains a wonderful fragrance by adding a few drops of perfume or essential oil to the wash cycle.

Secret Weapon:
A Cup of White Vinegar

This trick is so good it's surprising you don't find it prominently mentioned in the owners manual of every washing machine. Add 1 cup (250 ml) white vinegar to your washing machine's rinse cycle and you'll get benefits you never expected.

Makes laundry soft and fresh-smelling. You may not even need a liquid fabric softener.

Brightens things up. See the difference when you do small loads of white clothes, sheets and towels.

Sets color. Adding it will set the color of your newly dyed fabrics.

Reduces lint and static. Added to the last rinse, a cup of vinegar will keep these annoying laundry woes at bay.

3% hydrogen peroxide along the ring. Now wash in hot water as you normally would and make room in the closet for your old friend.

WHITEN CLOTHES WITHOUT BLEACH

Let your whites soak in a basin of hot water and lemon slices (tied in muslin) for 1 to 2 hours, then wash as usual. If clothes are particularly dingy, boil the water, turn off the heat, add your clothing and lemon slices, and soak overnight.

Insider Tip

To stop your neck from staining a shirt collar, wipe your neck with rubbing alcohol each morning before you dress.

Insider Tip

The old-fashioned power of sunlight helps brighten whites and gives them that wonderful fresh outdoor scent.

KEEP COLORS BRIGHT

That new cherry red shirt you just purchased is fantastic, but just think how faded the color will look after the shirt has been washed a few times. Add 1 teaspoon (5 ml) of pepper to the wash. Pepper keeps bright colors bright and prevents them from running, too. Another option to maintain bright colors is to add sugar to the rinse water so colored laundry comes out bright.

Take Care — Never hang your colored laundry to dry in bright sunlight, as the colors will fade.

STOP REDS FROM RUNNING

Unless you have a fondness for pink-tinted clothing, take this simple precaution to prevent red—or other brightly dyed—washable clothes from ruining your wash loads. Soak your new garments in a few cups of undiluted white vinegar for 10 to 15 minutes before their first washing. You'll never have to worry about running colors again!

BLACK SILK SECRET

Allow black silk to retain its shine by washing it with black tea and a little mild detergent.

Blacker Blacks, Darker Darks

Want to fight the fade? All you need are a few extra household ingredients.

For blacks, add 2 cups (500 ml) brewed coffee or tea to the rinse cycle.

For dark colors such as navy blue or plum, add 1 cup (250 ml) table salt to the rinse cycle.

For denim that will be slow to fade, soak jeans in salt water or a 50:50 solution of water and white vinegar before the first wash. Turn the jeans inside out before putting them in the machine and turn the temperature setting to cold.

Handy Hack

Washable velvet will shine after being laundered if you brush it down with a little salt.

FOR DELICATE FABRICS

Ordinary chlorine bleach can cause the iron in water to precipitate out into fabrics, leaving additional stains. For a mild, stain-free bleach, soak delicates in a mixture of lemon juice and baking soda for at least half an hour before washing.

WOOLENS SOFT TO THE TOUCH

Woolens will stay soft if you add a few drops of vinegar to the next-to-last rinse and a similar quantity of glycerin to the final rinse.

RESHAPE YOUR WOOLENS

Shrunken woolen sweaters and other items can sometimes be stretched back to their former size or shape after boiling them in a solution of 1 part vinegar to 2 parts water for around 25 minutes. Allow the garment to air-dry after you've finished stretching it.

FLUFF SWEATERS AFTER WASHING

Wool and acrylic sweaters can look flat and dull after washing, and sometimes a hint of laundry soap lingers in the fibers. Whether hand- or machine-washing, cut the soap and fluff up the fibers by adding ½ cup (125 ml) of white vinegar to the final rinse water.

STOP A SUDSY DISASTER

Ever put too much soap in a washing machine, or found that your child used dishwashing liquid in the dishwasher? When the suds start to emerge from the door of the machine, you may think they'll never stop. Put a halt to the proceedings by sprinkling salt over the mountain of bubbles. They'll quickly subside so you can clean up fast.

BOOST WITH A LITTLE LEMON

To remove unsightly rust and mineral discolorations from cotton T-shirts and underpants, pour 1 cup (250 ml) lemon juice into the washing machine during the wash cycle. The natural bleaching action of the juice will zap the stains and leave your clothes smelling fresh.

SAY BYE TO MOTHBALL SMELLS

If your clothes come out of storage reeking of mothballs, take heed: Adding ½ cup (125 ml) baking soda during your washing machine's rinse cycle will get rid of the smell.

POP PLUSHIES INTO THE MACHINE

Children's stuffed toys may be cute but they get mighty dusty. When it's time for a bath, place them in a pillowcase and throw it into the washing machine. The pillowcase will ensure they get a gentle but thorough wash. If any parts fall off the stuffed animals, they'll be caught in the pillowcase so you can reattach them after their wash.

CLEAN UP BABY VOMIT

Babies tend to regurgitate—and usually not at opportune moments. Never leave home without a small bottle of baking soda in your diaper bag. If your baby spits up on his or her (or your) shirt after feeding, simply brush off any solid matter, moisten a washcloth, dip it in a bit of baking soda and dab the spot. The odor (and the stain) will soon be gone.

WASH NEW BABY CLOTHES

Get all the chemicals out of newborn babies' clothing—without using any harsh detergents. Wash new baby clothes with some mild soap and ½ cup (125 ml) baking soda.

MAKE YOUR NEW CLOTHES READY TO WEAR

Remove the chemicals, dust, odor and whatever else from your brand-new or secondhand clothes by pouring 1 cup (250 ml) white vinegar into the wash cycle the first time you launder them.

 Keep apple cider vinegar out of the laundry. Using it to pretreat clothes or adding it to wash or rinse water may actually create stains rather than remove them. Use only distilled white vinegar for laundering.

DULL THE SHINE IN YOUR PANTS' SEAT

Want to get rid of that shiny seat on your dark pants or skirt? Just brush the area lightly with a soft old toothbrush dipped in equal parts white vinegar and water, and pat dry with a soft towel.

REMOVE CIGARETTE SMELL FROM SUITS

If you find yourself heading home with the lingering smell of cigarette smoke on your good suit or dress, you can remove the odor without having to take your clothes to the dry cleaner. Just add 1 cup (250 ml) vinegar to a bathtub filled with the hottest tap water you can get. Hang your garments above the steam and close the door. The smell should be gone after several hours.

TWO STARCH SUBSTITUTES

No need to run out to the store to buy starch to stiffen your shirt collars or restore body to shapeless clothing. Make your own by pouring 2 cups (500 ml) water into a jar and adding 2 tablespoons (30 ml) cornstarch. Screw the jar lid on tightly and shake well. Now pour the solution into a repurposed spray bottle for use when ironing. Another option is to add a cup (250 ml) of powdered milk to the final rinse cycle of the wash. Got milk? You've got shape.

RESTORE CRISPNESS TO LACE

If you have a lace scarf or shawl that's gone limp, wash it as you normally would and then dip it in a solution of 2 gallons (7.5 L) warm water and 1 cup (250 ml) Epsom salt. The salt will cling to the fibers and add body.

KETTLE-CLEAN YOUR FELT HAT

To deep-clean your wool felt hat, fill a teakettle with water, place it on the stove and bring it to a boil. Carefully hold the hat above the steam, rotating it as necessary. Brush with a dry toothbrush and let dry.

Handy Hack

Make your patent-leather bags or shoes look new again. Just dab on a little milk, let it dry and buff with a soft cloth.

FRESHEN A LAUNDRY HAMPER

Hampers are handy for keeping dirty laundry in one place, but they can get a little ripe when packed with soiled clothes. To prevent hamper smells, cut the foot off a pair of old pantyhose, fill it with baking soda, knot it and toss this makeshift odor-eater into the hamper. Replace the baking soda every month.

SLEEPING BAG TRICK

Sleeping bags tend to become a bit musty after a couple of uses, but you can freshen a bag by putting a bar of soap inside. Do it after you crawl out of the sleeping bag each morning, then zip the bag shut. The next time you slip in, remove the freshener and put it aside to use again, then drift off into sweet-smelling dreams.

GET THAT STAIN OUT!

KNOW WATER-SOLUBLE VS. PROTEIN

Water-soluble stains are the most common. All you'll need to remove them is tap water, at least when they are fresh. Treat protein-based stains (blood, mayonnaise or egg) with cold water. You can lift out many other water-soluble stains—including beer, orange and other fruit juices, black coffee or tea, and vomit—from your cotton-blend clothing by patting the spot with a cloth or towel moistened with undiluted white vinegar just before washing it. For large stains, you may want to soak the garment overnight in a solution of 3 parts vinegar to 1 part cold water before washing.

WORK FROM THE OUTSIDE IN

Don't work from the center, where the stain is deepest, to the outside. This can cause the stain to spread. Instead, start from the outer edges and work your way in. Try a solution of 2 parts water to 1 part rubbing alcohol. (Simply soaking your stained clothes overnight in warm water should help get stains out, too.)

UNSET OLD STAINS

Older, set-in stains will often come out in the wash after being pretreated with a solution of 3 tablespoons (45 ml) white vinegar and 2 tablespoons (30 ml) dishwashing liquid in a quart (1 L) of warm water. Rub the solution into the stain and blot it dry before washing.

Insider Tip

If possible, scrape a dried stain with a spoon or soften it with glycerin before treating it.

REMOVE A SCORCH MARK

Left a brown scorch on a dress shirt with the iron? It can happen in the blink of an eye. The cleanup won't be quite that fast, but it will be effective. Douse the

RUBBING ALCOHOL

scorch with water (presumably not on your ironing board) then rub a generous amount of cornstarch into the stain. When the cornstarch dries, the stain will rinse out with the powder.

GET RID OF BLOODSTAINS

Wash bloodstains on clothing immediately in cold water—hot water will cause the protein in the blood to congeal and attach firmly to the fibers. For stubborn stains, moisten the clothing in cold salt water. Dry bloodstains should be soaked in cold water, then treated with salt water or a solution of baking soda. When cleaning delicate fabrics, use a paste of water and potato flour. Test a hidden section of fabric first. If the color is unaffected, spread it on the stain, let it work for a few minutes, rub it off and rinse thoroughly.

SIMPLE METHOD FOR BLOODSTAINS

Apply 3% hydrogen peroxide directly to a fresh bloodstain on your clothing, rinse with fresh water and launder as usual.

Handy Hack

Another easy fix for an unsightly bloodstain is to soak it overnight in cola (yes, soda pop).

SPILLED COFFEE

Soak coffee stains on clothes immediately in cold salt water; alternatively, presoak the stain in a solution of 1 quart (1 L) water, 1 tablespoon (15 ml) white vinegar and 1 teaspoon (5 ml) laundry detergent.

FRUITY PROBLEM

Treat fruit stains while fresh by holding the soiled item over a bowl and pouring a little very hot water on it. Alternatively, soak it in buttermilk and wash as usual. For dried fruit stains, sprinkle with lemon juice and rinse after 30 minutes.

GRAVY BE GONE

Cover a gravy stain with baking soda, cornstarch, flour or salt, all of which soak up grease. After brushing the substance off, pour liquid laundry detergent and hot water directly onto the stain.

GO AWAY, GREASE!

Butter, mayonnaise, cooking oil and engine oil are among the substances that can leave grease stains. Promptly sprinkle them with cornstarch to absorb the grease and brush away the saturated starch. You can also try rubbing off stains using hot water mixed with a little dishwashing liquid to dissolve the grease. For delicate fabrics, place a paper towel on both sides of the stain and iron it. Stains are best removed from wool by rubbing with a little mineral water and a towel.

REMOVE GREASE SPOTS

Another option is to rub chalk on a grease spot on clothing or table linen and let it absorb the oil before you brush it off. If the stain lingers, rub chalk into it again before laundering. To get rid of ring-around-the-collar stains, you can mark the stains heavily with chalk before laundering. The chalk will absorb the oils that hold dirt in.

GUMMY SITUATION

Unfortunately, it is easy to pick up chewing gum stains on pants or skirts from park benches or restaurant chairs.

Chewing gum is, of course, highly annoying but fortunately is not difficult to remove, especially from denim. Place the item in a plastic bag and put it in the freezer, as you can scrape off frozen chewing gum quite easily. Brush off any residue before laundering the item as usual. If you do not have a freezer, apply ice cubes to the stain, then proceed as described once the gum has firmed up.

GET MILK STAINS OUT

Milk stains are relatively easy to remove. Simply treat fresh stains with warm soapy water. For dried milk stains, soak the item in warm soapy water before laundering it as usual.

NO MORE MUSTARD

Stir 1 tablespoon (15 ml) white vinegar and ½ teaspoon (2.5 ml) liquid laundry detergent into 1 quart (1 L) warm water. Sponge the solution on the stain and let air-dry. Before washing the garment, apply liquid detergent directly to the spot.

SOAK OUT RED TOMATO SAUCE

It's a brave soul who eats spaghetti while wearing a white shirt without a big napkin tucked into his collar. For an effective tomato sauce spot eradicator, combine ½ cup (125 ml) 3% hydrogen peroxide and 3 cups (750 ml) water. Soak

Red Wine Stain Relief

The wine tasted terrific last night, but the few drops on your slacks don't look all that great this morning. Club soda is a common antidote for red wine stains, but if that doesn't work, try one of these treatments:

Baking soda Heap baking soda onto the stain and let it sit for an hour or more to absorb the stain. Then shake off the baking soda and launder the garment.

Borax Dissolve 1 tablespoon (15 ml) of borax in 2 cups (500 ml) warm water. Submerge the stained part of the garment in the solution and soak for 1 minute, then toss the item into the washer.

Dishwashing liquid and vinegar Dilute your favorite dishwashing liquid and gently scrub it into the stain; rinse gently with water, then apply a drop of white vinegar. Pat dry and rinse again with water.

Hydrogen peroxide This works well to remove wine stains from clothing, so don't worry if you spill some while you quaff.

Salt and boiling water Pour a generous amount of salt on a still-wet stain and see if the salt turns pink as it soaks up the wine. If it doesn't, pour boiling water over the salt. In either case, wash the stained garment ASAP.

the stain in the solution for 30 minutes before laundering.

A TOAST TO CLUB SODA

The most successful way to get rid of stains is to treat them before they dry and become set in the fabric. If you're at a restaurant or a friend's home and food or drink drops onto your clothes, ask right away for a glass of club soda and a lint-free kitchen towel. Head to the restroom with the soda and apply as much as you can. Wait 1 minute, then blot the stain gently with the towel.

Make Ink Blotches Disappear

Frustrated by ink stains on your favorite clothes? There are a variety of ways to get those blemishes out. Decide which works best for you!

You can treat fresh ink stains by sprinkling the stained area repeatedly with salt and rinsing under running water.

Try drizzling ink stains with lemon juice before laundering.

Remove ink stains from colored clothes with an overnight milk bath. Soak the garment in milk overnight and machine wash as usual the next day.

Put 2 to 3 tablespoons (30 to 45 ml) cornstarch in a bowl and then stir in whole milk until you

have a thick paste. Cover an ink stain with the paste and let it sit for 3 to 4 hours. Then brush off the paste and wash the item.

Another paste to try out is 2 tablespoons (30 ml) cream of tartar mixed with 2 tablespoons (30 ml) lemon juice for those nasty ink spots.

Soak the spot in rubbing alcohol a few minutes. Use an eyedropper or similar tool to circle the ink spot before applying it to the stain itself. This will prevent the spot from spreading. Blot the spot with paper towels to remove as much ink as possible, then put the garment into the wash.

Yet another way to rid a pen-ink stain is to treat it by first wetting it with some white vinegar, then rubbing in a paste of 2 parts vinegar to 3 parts cornstarch. Let the paste thoroughly dry before washing garment.

GRASSY GREEN STREAKS

Treat fresh grass stains by applying a halved potato to the stain to allow the starch to dissolve it, then wash as usual. Soak older grass stains on white fabrics in a mixture of 1 part egg white and 1 part glycerin before washing. Two other options include soaking grass stains in full-strength white vinegar, or brushing non-gel, non-whitening toothpaste directly onto the stain.

Handy Hack

Rub a mud stain with a peeled slice of raw potato, and then soak the garment in cold water for at least 15 minutes.

RECIPE: RED CLAY STAIN REMOVER

If you garden in an area with clay soil, you know all too well how its red color stains your clothes. Set aside an old pair of jeans just to garden in. When they're caked with mud, use this simple recipe to keep stains off the clothes you wash with them.

Vinegar
Table salt

Drape the muddy jeans over the back of a garden chair and rinse vigorously with a garden hose.

In a small jar, add vinegar to the salt, a little at a time, to make a paste. Rub the paste into the mud stains, allow to sit for 20 minutes, then launder as usual.

CLEAR AWAY CRAYON

Somehow or other, kids often manage to get crayon marks on their clothing. You can easily get these stains off by rubbing them with an old toothbrush soaked in undiluted vinegar before washing the item.

WASH OUT MAKEUP WITH BAKING SODA

If you've spilled foundation makeup on your blouse, go to the kitchen and grab a box of trusty baking soda. Sprinkle the powder onto the stain until it's completely covered and press it gently into the fabric. Wet a nailbrush or a toothbrush and lightly brush the spot. If any makeup remains, repeat the process until all traces have disappeared.

THE BREAD TREATMENT

Blot up foundation makeup marks on washable fabrics with fresh white bread kneaded into a ball. The bread treatment should also erase pencil marks on woolen and washable clothing. Resist the temptation to use the pencil's eraser to rub out the marks, which in most cases will only make them look much worse.

LIPSTICK SMEAR REMOVER

Bread also works to get out lipstick. Tear out the doughy center of the bread and knead it into a ball, then blot the smear repeatedly with the dough until the stain lifts from the fabric. Now wash the garment. The dough ball is also safe to use on lipstick marks on no-wash woolen clothing.

TOUGH LIPSTICK STAINS

To remove stubborn lipstick stains, dab them with eucalyptus oil, letting it soak in before washing. Boil white table napkins, handkerchiefs or washcloths marked by lipstick stains.

OIL SPOT SOLUTIONS

Remove oil stains from textiles by sprinkling them immediately with cornstarch, allowing the starch to soak up the oil, then brushing it out. Baking soda is another alternative. Most fresh oil stains can also be scrubbed with hot water (over 140°F) and dishwashing liquid, but note that synthetic fibers do not tolerate high temperatures. Use a different approach for dried oil stains. If they are on delicate fabric, cover the stain with parchment paper and iron over the stain. Have the setting just hot

enough so that the oil melts and is
soaked up by the paper.

REMOVE SWEAT MARKS

Chlorine bleach makes pit stains even
worse. A great home remedy is to mix
1 part baking soda to 1 part hydrogen
peroxide to 1 part water. Rub the solution
on the stains and let it sit for at least
30 minutes before washing. Another
option to remove those yellowing
underarm stains from shirts and blouses
is to simply scrub them with a mixture
of equal parts lemon juice and water.

Handy Hack Got deodorant stains?
Get them out of your
washable shirts and
blouses easily by gently
rubbing the area with undiluted
vinegar before laundering.

STEAM SUEDE

Whether you discover a stain on your
suede shoes or your suede jacket, you
won't be happy. Bring a smile back to
your face quickly by rubbing the stain
gently with the fine side of an emery
board, then holding the suede item
over steam from a pan. The stain will
disappear! You can use the emery
board again to freshen the nap.

RECIPE: PERSPIRATION STAIN REMOVER

*You can also try this homemade
remedy for sweat stains on fabric.*

1	cup (250 ml) white vinegar
¼	cup (60 ml) salt
8	cups (2 L) warm water

Mix the ingredients in a bucket
and soak the garment for 1 hour
before washing.

BRUSH OFF YOUR SUEDE

To eliminate a fresh grease spot on a
suede jacket or skirt, gently brush it with
a soft toothbrush dipped in white vinegar.
Let the spot air-dry, then brush with a
suede brush. Repeat if necessary. You
can also generally tone up suede items
by lightly wiping them with a sponge
dipped in vinegar.

Handy Hack Rub gently with an eraser
not only to remove minor
stains and marks from
suede shoes and bags,
but also to fluff up the suede fibers.

SAY BYE TO TAR

Try rubbing tar stains with lard before washing the item. For an extra boost, add 2 tablespoons (30 ml) baking soda to the laundry detergent. Oil, tar and grass stains can also be treated with a few drops of eucalyptus oil.

ELIMINATE URINE STAINS

After blotting up as much urine as possible from the stain, pour club soda over the stained area and immediately blot again. The club soda will get rid of the stain and help reduce odor.

WAX ON FABRIC?

Scratch off a wax spot, place a paper towel under and over the spot and iron until all excess wax is absorbed. If necessary, replace the paper towel. Remove any remaining stain from colored wax by dabbing it with rubbing alcohol, always working from the outside in.

GET RUST OUT OF YOUR COTTON CLOTHING

To remove a rust stain from your cotton work clothes (or any cotton item), first moisten the rust spot with some full-strength vinegar and rub in a bit of salt. If it's warm outdoors, let it dry in the sunlight (otherwise a sunny window will do), then toss it into the wash.

VANISHING SPOTS

Out of stain stick and ready to do a load of laundry? Don't worry—grab your dishwashing liquid and get to work. Gently rub the liquid on the stained fabric, let it sit and then machine wash the item as usual. You'll find the stains will disappear.

REMOVE STAINS OF AN UNKNOWN ORIGIN

Can't tell what a stain is, but still want to try removing it? Try this surefire mixture. Mix 1 teaspoon (5 ml) 3% hydrogen peroxide with a little cream of tartar or a dab of non-gel toothpaste. Rub the paste on the stain with a soft cloth and rinse. The stain should be gone.

FABRIC SOFTENER TIPS

VINEGAR: FABRIC SOFTENER PLUS

Who would have guessed that a single cup of an everyday staple—white vinegar, which costs almost nothing—could do everything that many people use a fabric softener, a color setter, a cleaner and a bleach to do? Just add 1 cup (250 ml) distilled white vinegar to your washing machine's rinse cycle. It will help to eliminate bacteria in the wash, set the color of newly dyed fabrics, keep clothes lint- and static-free, brighten small loads of white clothes, and remove the need for fabric softeners.

Take Care
Don't add fabric softener while washing towels. It can make them less absorbent. If you already doused them in the stuff before reading this, you can bring them back by adding a cup of distilled vinegar to the rinse cycle.

Take Care
Avoid using fabric softener with microfiber fabrics. Softeners attach to the surface of the fiber and prevent it from functioning as intended, as far as moisture wicking and breathability are concerned.

MAKE YOUR OWN FABRIC SOFTENER

There's no need to spend money on commercial fabric softeners when you probably have all the ingredients you need to make your own. See for yourself with this simple recipe. You can also use this solution to make a fabric softener sheet to toss in the dryer. Just dilute with water, dip in a washcloth and wring it out, and add the washcloth to your load of wet clothes.

- 2 cups (500 ml) white vinegar
- 2 cups (500 ml) baking soda
- 4 cups (1 L) water

Combine ingredients in a gallon-size (4 L) pail or pot and stir to dissolve the baking soda.

Pour the solution into an old plastic bottle with a lid. (An old liquid detergent bottle works.)

To use, add ¼ cup (60 ml) softener to the washer's final rinse cycle.

WHEN IRONING

GOT A GUNKED-UP IRON?

If you find that you have a gunky iron, lay out a piece of aluminum foil and iron it. The buildup should stick to the foil after a few passes. That gunk comes from touching a hot iron to synthetic fabric, causing the fibers to melt and coat the iron in the liquid material. Every time you fire up the iron from that point on, it will melt a bit of the gunk and transfer it to anything else it touches—until you fix it.

AVOID DESCALING AN IRON

If your iron doesn't have a scale filter and you want to save yourself the trouble of descaling it, use distilled water (available from hardware stores and supermarkets).

FLUSH YOUR IRON'S INTERIOR

To eliminate mineral deposits and prevent corrosion on your steam iron, give it an occasional cleaning by filling the reservoir with undiluted white vinegar. Place the iron in an upright position, switch on the steam setting and let the vinegar steam through it for 5 to 10 minutes. Refill the chamber with clean water and repeat. Finally, give the water chamber a good rinsing with cold, clean water.

UNCLOG IRON PORTS

If your iron doesn't emit steam the way it should, minerals may be clogging the steam ports. Unplug your iron, let it cool and then try cleaning out the ports on the bottom with the end of a straightened paper clip.

CLEAN YOUR IRON'S METAL SOLEPLATE

It seems to happen on a regular basis. No matter how careful you are while ironing, something melts onto the iron, forming a rough surface that is difficult to remove. Salt crystals are the answer. Turn your iron to high, sprinkle table salt on a section of newspaper on your ironing board and run the hot iron over the salt. You'll iron away the bumps.

SCORCHED SOLEPLATE

To remove scorch marks from the soleplate of your iron, scrub it with a paste made by heating equal parts vinegar and salt in a small saucepan. Use a rag dipped in clean water to wipe away the remaining residue.

Handy Hack

So your ready-to-wear shirt is full of wrinkles and you don't have time to wash it again. Turn on the iron and wrap an ice cube in a soft cloth. Rub this over the wrinkle just before you iron and the shirt will smooth out.

SPRAY AWAY WRINKLES

In a perfect world, laundry would emerge from the dryer freshly pressed. Until that day, you can often get the wrinkles out of clothes after drying by misting them with a solution of 1 part vinegar to 3 parts water. Once you're sure you didn't miss a spot, hang them up and let them air-dry. You may find that this approach works better for some clothes than ironing, and it's certainly a lot gentler on the garment fabric.

DON'T IRON DELICATE CURTAINS

Sheer curtains, which are usually made from synthetic fabrics, should be washed on your machine's delicate cycle with a gentle spin. Hang them back up while they are still damp and the sheer fabric will dry crease-free without the need for ironing. If the weather permits, leave the window open to allow the moisture to escape the room.

SHARPEN YOUR CREASES

You'll find that the creases in freshly ironed clothes will come out a lot neater if you lightly spray them with equal parts water and vinegar before ironing them. For truly sharp creases in slacks and dress shirts, first dampen the garment using a cloth moistened in a solution

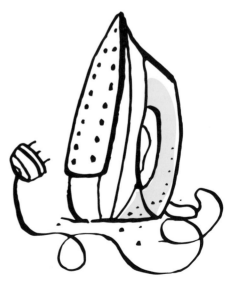

Undo a Scorch (Fast!)

It's your anniversary and your first gift to your wife is to do the ironing before she awakens. Won't she be surprised! You bet, but not so much by your generous act as by the scorch on her pale blue blouse. Who knew the iron heated up so quickly? Lucky for you, scorch marks don't have to be permanent. Here are four techniques to try:

For white cottons Take a cotton cloth dampened with 3% hydrogen peroxide and dab at the scorch until it's gone.

For colored cottons Wet a lint-free cloth with 3% hydrogen peroxide or white vinegar and lay it over the scorch. Press with the iron on low.

For all washable cottons Cut an onion in half, rub it on the scorch, soak overnight in cold water and then wash.

For woolens Dampen the scorch with water and dab cornstarch onto it. Let sit 20 to 30 minutes and then brush off.

of 1 part white vinegar and 2 parts water. Then place a brown paper bag over the crease and start ironing.

MAKE OLD HEMLINES DISAPPEAR

When you want to make unsightly needle marks from an old hemline disappear for good, simply moisten the area with a cloth dipped in equal parts vinegar and water, and place it under the garment before you start ironing.

Insider Tip If you usually pack a travel iron—just in case you end up in a motel that doesn't provide irons and ironing boards—it's a cinch to make your own on-the-road ironing board. Simply fill a pillowcase with a short stack of newspapers, keeping it as level as possible. Place it on a countertop or the floor and get pressing.

AROUND
THE HOME

CLEANING MADE EASY

SPRAY IT PROUD!

Why use commercial cleaner when you can make an all-purpose wash that's cheap, simple and green to boot? In a repurposed spray bottle, mix 2 parts water with 1 part white vinegar. You can spritz it on almost anything including grease spots, spills and bathroom surfaces.

Take Care Never use acidic substances (such as vinegar or citric acid) on marble or limestone as well as some types of grout. Acid will attack the surface, leaving it dull and blotchy. Some people recommend polishing marble with linseed oil, but this is not a good idea either as it can leave spots on the surface.

WASHING SODA FOR CLEANING

As far as cleaning products go, washing soda (sodium carbonate) is as effective as it is inexpensive. Simply dissolve in warm water or, for tough grime, sprinkle a little powder directly onto a damp cloth.

MAKE METAL HARDWARE SHINE

The best way to clean handles, hinges and other metal hardware will depend on the material from which they are made. Warm water with a few drops of dishwashing liquid is all you need for stainless steel or chrome hardware. Polish with a soft, dry cloth to finish.

Take Care Never use vinegar to clean tarnished brass hardware as the acid will attack the metal.

POLISH METAL AND MARBLE

To make metal shine like new, put some chalk dust on a damp cloth and wipe. (You can make chalk dust by pulverizing pieces of chalk.) Buff with a soft cloth for an even shinier finish. Wipe marble with a damp, soft cloth dipped in powdered chalk. Rinse with clear water and dry thoroughly.

COLA DOES THE JOB

Although it's best to use new nuts and bolts, you don't necessarily have to throw away fasteners that have gone a bit rusty. Try putting them in a glass of cola and leaving overnight. Cola drinks contain phosphoric acid, which reacts with iron oxide (rust) to form a stable protective

DIY CITRUS CLEANER

If you like commercial orange cleaners, you'll love this fresh citrus-scented vinegar spray. You can also deodorize a room by setting out a small bowl of citrus vinegar.

    Zest from 1 orange, grapefruit, lemon or lime
3   **cups (750 ml) white vinegar**
1   **clean qt. (1 L) container with lid**
1   **clean 32-oz. (1 L) repurposed spray bottle**

Combine the citrus zest and vinegar in the container with lid. Fasten the lid and store mixture in a cupboard for 2 weeks, giving it an occasional shake.

Remove the zest from the container, then strain the vinegar and return it to the container.

To use as a spray cleaner, pour 1 cup (250 ml) of citrus vinegar into the bottle and fill with water.

To clean linoleum floors, add 1 cup (250 ml) citrus vinegar to 2 gallons (8 L) water.

barrier. It's a trick that can give new life to all kinds of rusty old hardware.

RUST BUSTERS

Dip a rag into a paste made from 4 tablespoons (60 ml) salt and 2 tablespoons (30 ml) lemon juice to remove rust spots on chrome and other metallic surfaces. Brush rust stains on porcelain with toothpaste (tool of choice: old toothbrush).

CREATE YOUR OWN SOFT SCRUB

Got a surface that needs gentle cleaning, such as your elderly cast-iron tub or perhaps your brand-new designer sink? Make an effective cleanser that's devoid of harshness by mixing 2 teaspoons (10 ml) white vinegar with 2 teaspoons (10 ml) cream of tartar. Rub and scrub with a sponge, then rinse with warm water and buff dry.

KEEP PIPES CLEAR

Pour boiling water down the drain from time to time to help keep your pipes clear. It's kinder to the environment, as it can save the need to resort to chemical drain cleaners to clear a blockage. What's more, chemical drain cleaners don't always work and they can damage plumbing.

Hydrogen Peroxide:
Do's and Don'ts

DO NOT USE HYDROGEN PEROXIDE FOR:

Cleaning colored fabrics—it will bleach the color.

Cleaning metal items, such as food and water dishes for your pet or cages—there's a chance it could make metal rust faster.

Cleaning deep cuts—it can be used sparingly on small cuts and scrapes, but it can kill healthy bacteria and slow the healing process for deep cuts.

WHEN YOU USE HYDROGEN PEROXIDE:

Wear protective gloves—while it is a natural substance, it can still burn your skin.

Do not mix it with vinegar, ammonia or bleach—the combination could produce dangerous fumes.

Keep it safely out of the reach of children.

CLEAN YOUR COINS

Who wants dirty money? If coin collecting is your hobby, use cola to clean your stash. Place the coins in a small dish and soak in cola for a shimmering shine. Of course, you shouldn't do this with rare and valuable coins.

INK MARKS ON A DOLL'S FACE?

Many favorite dolls have been given an ink-pen makeover by an overzealous, underage beautician. You can undo the handiwork by rubbing butter on the pen stains and leaving the doll face-up in the sun for a few days. Then wash it off with soap and water.

WHAT DOLLS AND PLAYING CARDS HAVE IN COMMON

Dolls and other decorative items made of fabric are not easy to clean. You can try dabbing at the fabric laboriously with a damp cloth, but a simpler, more effective method is to place the dolls in a plastic bag with a teaspoon (5 ml) of baking soda. Give the bag a good shake and then brush the powder off the fabric. The cleaning properties of baking soda enable it to remove surface dirt. You can also use the same technique to freshen up a deck of playing cards that have started to stick together after prolonged use.

RECIPE: ALL-PURPOSE CLEANING AGENT

Some professional cleaners prefer to use a cleaning agent made from combining the following:

- 1   qt. (1 L) warm water
- 1   tsp. (5 ml) delicate laundry detergent
- 1   tsp. (5 ml) vinegar

Mix all ingredients well to create plenty of suds and then use with a cleaning cloth.

REFRESH STUFFED ANIMALS

To clean a stuffed toy animal, rub a bit of cornstarch on the toy, wait about 5 minutes and brush it clean. Or place the stuffed animal (or a few small ones) in a bag. Sprinkle cornstarch into the bag, close it tightly and shake. Now brush the stuffed toy clean and dispose of the cornstarch and the bag.

WHITEN PIANO KEYS

If you wonder how your piano keys got so yellow, don't despair: You can restore the whiteness in a few simple ways. Use a soft cloth to rub the keys with lemon juice and salt or with a 50:50 mix of rubbing alcohol and water; or apply mayonnaise and gently scrub with a soft cloth or soft toothbrush. Whichever method you choose, prevent seepage by holding a piece of cardboard between the keys as you work your way down the keyboard. Wipe off each key with a slightly damp cloth before moving on to the next one. Let the keys air-dry—and then sit down and take it away, maestro!

CLEAR FLOWER VASE RESIDUE

Once your beautiful bouquet is gone, the souvenir it leaves behind is not the kind of reminder you want: deposits of minerals on the vase interior. Reach

CLOUDY GLASS VASE REMEDY

You can combat serious dirt or clouding on glassware with a salt and vinegar paste.

⅓ cup (80 ml) salt
2 Tbsp. (30 ml) vinegar

Mix the salt and vinegar to form a paste. Spread the paste on the inside of the vase using a finger or a soft brush. Let it sit for 15 to 20 minutes, then wipe off the paste and rinse the vase with clear water.

inside the vase, rub the offending ring of deposits with salt, and wash with soapy water. If your hand won't fit inside, fill the vase with a strong solution of salt and water, shake it or brush gently with a bottle brush, then wash. This should clear away the residue.

After leaded crystal vases have been washed, buff these vases dry with a chamois.

The Home Library

Don't overlook cleaning the books in your bookcase. Keep your favorite hardcover tomes in bestselling shape and you'll have them forever. Here's how:

To dry a damp book, fan out the pages and sprinkle on cornstarch to soak up the moisture. Let sit for 5 to 6 hours and then brush off the stuff.

To get rid of insects that reside in books, place an infested book in a plastic bag and pop it into the freezer for a day or two. No more bugs or larvae.

To freshen up a musty-smelling volume, pour some clean cat litter into a paper bag and keep the book in the bag for a week or so. Then remove the book and brush off any litter.

Mildewed pages? Wipe away the mold with a cloth barely moistened with a solution of 1 part white vinegar to 8 parts water. To dry, open the book to the affected pages and place it in the sun; let it sunbathe for no more than half an hour or the paper will fade and yellow.

Use a clean, soft paintbrush to dust one book at a time, brushing the covers and the outer edges of the pages. Do not dust a shelf of books with a feather duster, which will only redistribute most of the dust on the volumes.

ALGAE IN VASE

To combat algae growth in a vase, add a handful of black tea leaves and douse them with vinegar. Tip the vase back and forth until the green coating of the algae disappears.

FRESHEN A REPURPOSED BOTTLE

Want to use that nice wine bottle for cold water or that cold cream pot for a homemade cosmetic? That's a great idea, unless you can't get rid of the scent of whatever went before. Squirt yellow mustard into the bottle, half fill with warm water and slosh gently. Let it sit for 15 minutes, then rinse and wash. The bottle will smell of...nothing.

Handy Hack

You can't keep a good lookout for trees and other skiers through snow goggles that fog up during a downhill descent. Rub raw potato over goggles before getting on the ski lift and the ride down should be crystal clear.

SPECTACLE SOLUTION

Why buy a special spray to clean your eyeglasses when you have vinegar in the cabinet? Spritz your specs with white vinegar and polish with a soft cloth. It will work just as well as that tiny, overpriced bottle of cleaner.

RUB EYEGLASSES THE RIGHT WAY

When used to clean eyeglass lenses, tissues and paper towels can scratch the surface over time. Instead, cut 4-inch (10 cm) squares of soft, 100% cotton cloth. Store one in your eyeglasses case, one on your desk or by the bed—anywhere you might need to give your

Mineral Deposit Remover

If you live in an area with hard water, sooner or later you'll notice that your coffee maker takes longer to brew and the coffee doesn't taste as good, your carpet steamer doesn't work as well as it did, and your steam iron may stop steaming. Here's how to make them all like new again.

To clean coffee makers, steam-cleaning machines and steam irons, pour ½ cup (125 ml) white vinegar into the water reservoir (or more as needed to fill the reservoir), turn the machine on and allow it to run until all of the vinegar passes through.

Then fill the reservoir with clean water and run the entire reservoir of clean water through the machine to rinse out the vinegar residue. With coffee makers, repeat rinsing stage if needed.

specs a rub. Gently polishing with these unhemmed squares will give eyeglasses longer life and give you a much clearer field of vision!

NEW LIFE FOR BASEBALL MITT

Recondition an old mitt with olive oil and you'll bring softness and shine to that hard-worn old leather. Pour oil on a rag and then work it into the glove well, rubbing into cracks and crevices. Use a clean rag to buff off any excess, and then fly balls had better watch out!

CLEAN A COOLER

You're not the only family that ever forgot a pack of hot dogs in a cooler after you came home from a trip. But you don't have to throw away an expensive item just because of one mistake. Clean out the cooler and pour in a large can of tomato juice, undiluted. Rub it up the sides of the interior and under the lid with a sponge, then close the lid and let it sit in a cool place for a couple of days. Rinse and wash with dish soap and water and dry thoroughly. Sprinkle the inside with a little baking soda before you put it into storage.

GLUE BEGONE

You don't need to buy small bottles of expensive glue removers—you can wipe

FRESH-SMELLING MULTIPURPOSE CLEANER

This formula has a clean smell and works hard, despite its inexpensive ingredients. You can buy liquid castile soap at health food stores.

3½	cups (875 ml) hot water
½	cup (125 ml) white or apple cider vinegar
1	tsp. (5 ml) borax
1	tsp. (5 ml) washing soda
1	tsp. (5 ml) liquid castile soap
1	clean 32-oz. (1 L) repurposed spray bottle

Fill spray bottle first with hot water; then add vinegar, borax, washing soda and liquid castile soap. Shake well before using.

Spray on non-stone countertops, kitchen appliances and fixtures, and tile or painted surfaces.

Wipe down with a clean cloth or damp sponge.

stubborn adhesive tags from store-bought products with a little household staple. Dip a clean cloth into white vinegar and rub it over the glue spot until it loosens. Remove glue with a dry corner of the cloth. Use a plastic spatula to lift any stubborn spots. Rinse the spot with a clean, damp cloth, and then polish with a dry cloth.

TAKE OFF A PRICE TAG

Rub on a dab of peanut butter, let it sit for a few minutes, and then wipe clean with a paper towel. The peanut butter wipes clean in seconds, and so do the remains of the glue.

THE ALL-PURPOSE TOOTHBRUSH

You can use old toothbrushes to clean a host of diverse items and small or hard-to-reach areas and crevices. Use them to clean artificial plants, costume jewelry, combs, shower tracks, crevices between tiles and the area around faucets. They're good for computer keyboards, can opener blades and around stove burners. And

don't forget the seams on shoes where leather meets the sole.

BURNISH YOUR SCISSORS

When your scissor blades get sticky or grimy, don't use water to wash them off; you're far more likely to rust the fastener that holds the blades together—or even the blades—than get them clean. Instead, wipe down the blades with a cloth dipped in full-strength white vinegar, and dry them off with a rag or dish towel.

BROKEN GLASS?

Sweeping or vacuuming is not the most reliable way to pick up tiny fragments of broken glass. It's better to use an adhesive lint roller, the same kind for removing pet hairs. In a pinch, a slice of fresh bread will also do the job. Obviously, throw it in the trash when you're done!

SHAKE UP ARTIFICIAL FLOWERS

Authentic silk flowers are actually pretty rare these days. Most are now made of nylon or some other man-made material. Whether they're silk or something else, you can easily freshen them up by placing them in a paper bag with ¼ cup (60 ml) salt. Give the bag a few gentle shakes and your flowers will emerge as clean as the day you purchased them.

GOT A GLASS-FRONT FIREPLACE?

If the glass in front of your fireplace or woodstove is blackened with soot and smoke, it's time for baking soda. Crumple a sheet of newspaper, wet it in water and dip it in baking soda. Scrub the glass—the black stuff will come right off. Wipe with a damp cloth. You can use the same technique to get soot off the glazed bricks lining the fireplace.

 Insider Tip Clean the tiles or bricks around the fireplace with a scrub brush moistened with white vinegar.

EASY FIREPLACE CLEANUP

When you're ready to turn in for the night but the fire is still glowing in the hearth, douse the flames with salt. The fire will burn out more quickly, so you'll wind up with less soot than if you let it smolder. Cleanup is easier, too, because the salt helps the ash and residue gather into easy sweepings.

TAMP DOWN THE ASHES

A fireplace is a delight—until it's time to sweep out the ashes the next day, kicking up a cloud of dust and making you cough. Sprinkle the dead ashes liberally with moist coffee grounds and then sweep away. The dampness and weight of the grounds prevents clouds of dust dancing around your living room as you clean.

HOW TO CLEAN THE DOOR OF A WOOD HEATER

There's no need to buy expensive products to clean the glass door of your wood heater. When the door is cool, simply dampen a sheet of paper towel, dab it in some pale-colored wood ash, then rub it over the glass to remove the layer of soot and brown-colored deposits. You will be amazed by how easily this works. The secret is that potash (potassium carbonate) contained in the ash acts as a natural cleaning product.

READY YOUR AC FOR THE SEASON

Before air-conditioning window units go in, the filters should be washed. Brush off obvious dirt and dust, then lay the filters in a basin of water with several tablespoons (45 to 60 ml) baking soda mixed in. Swish them in the water to clean, then rinse and dry in hot sun before replacing in the unit.

DEGREASE GRATES, FANS AND AIR-CONDITIONER GRILLES

Even in the cleanest of homes, air-conditioner grilles, heating grates and fan blades eventually develop a layer of dust and grease and grime. To clean, wipe them over with full-strength white vinegar. Use an old toothbrush to work the vinegar into the tight spaces on air-conditioner grilles and exhaust fans.

KEEP FILTERS CLEAN

An air-conditioner or humidifier filter can quickly become inundated with dust, soot, pet hair and even potentially harmful bacteria. Every 10 days or so, you can clean your filter in equal parts white vinegar and warm water. Let the filter soak in the solution for an hour and simply squeeze it dry before using. If your filters are particularly dirty, let them soak overnight to dislodge stubborn grime.

SCOUR BARBECUE GRATES

Keep your barbecue grate in top condition by making a soft paste of ¼ cup (60 ml) baking soda and ¼ cup (60 ml) water. Apply the paste with a wire brush and let dry for 15 minutes. Then wipe it down with a dry cloth and place the grate over hot coals for at least 15 minutes to burn off remaining residue before placing any food on it.

Handy Hack

Grilling can be thrilling—until it comes time to clean the grill. If you don't have a scouring pad around, just ball up some aluminum foil and use it to scrape grime off the grill.

STOP FLARE-UPS

One of the best ways to prevent a grease flare-up when grilling meat is to place a couple of slices of white bread in the drip pan to absorb the grease. It will also cut down on the amount of smoke produced.

DUSTING DONE RIGHT

Preventing a mess is better than cleaning it up afterward. Avoid leaving windows open for too long to stop excessive dirt and dust from blowing in.

CLEANING CLOTH SYSTEM

No one likes the idea of the dining room table being wiped down with the same cloth you've just used to clean the bathroom. To prevent this, use a four-colored system for your cleaning cloths: reserve red for the toilet and surrounding floor and tiles; yellow for the rest of the bathroom including basin, bathtub, tiles and bathroom mirrors; green in the kitchen for the countertops, dishwasher and fridge; and blue for living areas, chairs, shelves and so on.

SOCKS AS MITTS

Save those old or solo socks to use as cleaning mitts. Slip them on and they'll be great for cleaning corners and crevices.

TOP TO BOTTOM

When cleaning, move around the room slowly so as not to stir up dust unnecessarily and work from top to bottom. Start with light fixtures, lamps, picture frames and the top surfaces of tall furniture, then move on to surfaces at eye level and below. End with windowsills and baseboards. Use a long duster to do high dusting and under furniture where your vacuum can't reach.

FINISH DUSTING WITH THE VACUUM CLEANER

Vacuum upholstered furniture first, then baseboards and other pieces of furniture, and finally the floor, starting from the farthest corner of the room and working toward the door. To get the best results, go over each area with a series of vertical strokes followed by a series of horizontal ones. Don't forget to use a crevice tool to get into edges and corners where dust and germs lurk.

DIY FILTER TO AVOID TINY ITEMS

A vacuum nozzle is a great way to clean dust from the tops of bureaus or the edges of shelves, unless you sweep up earrings, marbles or other tiny items. Fix a square of cheesecloth over the end of the nozzle with a strong rubber band and clean away! The cheesecloth filters out the items you don't want sucked up but lets the dust through.

EXTEND VACUUM REACH WITH THIS SECRET

Can't reach that cobweb on the ceiling with your regular vacuum cleaner attachment? Try using a long, empty cardboard tube to extend the reach. You can even crush the end of the cardboard tube to create a crevice tool. Use duct tape to make the connection airtight.

CLEAR OUT COBWEBS

There's a cobweb way up high in the corner of your dining room. Before you take a broom to it, cover the bristles of the broom completely with an old pillowcase. Now you can wipe away the cobweb without scratching the wall paint or leaving a dirty mark.

It's also easier to remove the cobweb from the pillowcase than to pull it out of the broom bristles.

Handy Hack

Cobwebs in hard-to-reach ceiling corners can be tough to reach with a vacuum cleaner or a broom. Try throwing a piece of scrunched-up newspaper into the corner to remove them.

GET IN THE CRACKS

As with auto detailers who clean around the radio dial, a cotton swab or toothpick will let you "detail" areas in your house that are hard to clean. Dip the tip in a little rubbing alcohol and run it around the dials on your stove, the cracks in the phone, the lettering on your fridge—anywhere those fine lines can accumulate dirt.

DUST DELICATE ITEMS

A soft paintbrush is ideal for cleaning china figurines, chandeliers, lampshades—anything that you don't want to rub with a cloth. It's perfect for getting into the cracks and crevices of sculpted items, and it won't damage delicate parts.

Don't Put Up with Dust Mites

Nobody ever truly sleeps alone. Dust mites are all over our homes, wherever there is food and moisture. Their feces trigger allergic reactions like red watery eyes, a runny nose or even breathing difficulties. Some easy precautions will help to alleviate the problem. Regular vacuuming is your first defense.

Dust mites love down comforters. If you have a dust-mite allergy, use comforters with a synthetic filling and wash regularly at 140°F. Mites also live inside mattresses, closets and crevices in the floor. Vacuum and wipe these thoroughly and frequently.

Wall-to-wall carpets are not ideal if you have allergies. Replace with smooth floors and have only rugs that can be easily removed for cleaning. Be sure your vacuum cleaner has a HEPA filter so that you aren't blowing the mites and their feces around the rooms.

Insider Tip

A soft makeup brush is an ideal tool for removing dust from decorative picture or mirror frames. Use a really soft brush designed for applying blush.

TINY TREASURES TRICK

Find a pair of soft fabric garden gloves and put them on the next time you dust your knickknacks. Clean your treasures with your fingers. You'll have more control over the cleaning—meaning you'll be less likely to damage a knickknack.

PLASTER POINTERS

Dust plaster moldings and decorations regularly, preferably with a feather duster. Wet-wash plaster only when necessary. First check that the finish is solid enough, then spray it with a little soap and water so that you're able to reach even the cracks. Finally, spray with a small amount of clean water and dab up all liquid with a dry cloth.

DUST-FREE CEILING FAN

All you need for a ceiling fan cleanup is a ladder, an old cotton sock and a bucket of soapy water. Stir 1 teaspoon (5 ml) dishwashing liquid into 1 gallon (4 L) water. Dip the sock into the water and wring it out. Slip the sock over your hand, climb the ladder and rub your stockinged hand over each blade. Take care to clean the blades on both sides—the heaviest dust layer is on the top. The dust will be transferred directly to the damp sock, not to the air. A breeze, no?

Handy Hack

Grab an old pillowcase and place it over a ceiling fan blade. Slowly pull off the pillowcase. Repeat for each blade. The blades get dusted and the collected dust stays in the pillowcase instead of parachuting to the floor.

BLOW AWAY FROM BOOKS

Never use a cloth to dust books as you will only push the dust between the pages. It's better to blow the dust away (through an open window), then open the book and snap it shut to get rid of any dust inside. If this seems too laborious, use your vacuum cleaner's soft brush attachment to clean a whole shelf of books at one time.

HAIR DRYER = DUST BUSTER

A hair dryer can do more than blow-dry your hair. In fact, there is a whole range of uses for this humble household appliance. Use the cool air setting to blow dust off books, ornaments and other surfaces, and small objects. To prevent the dust from just being blown somewhere else inside, it's best to use this technique at an open window or on a balcony.

RADIATOR BUILDUP

Cast-iron radiators around the home have a tendency to become unsightly dust catchers. To clean them, hang a large, damp cloth behind each radiator and use a blow-dryer on its highest, coolest setting to blow dust and hidden dirt onto the cloth.

Insider Tip

Stair balustrades, whether made of wood, wrought iron or stainless steel, can be wiped down with a damp cloth.

BRIGHTEN AN OIL PAINTING

You wouldn't want to try this with a valuable oil painting, or with any museum-quality painting for that matter, but you can clean off everyday dust and grime that collects on an oil

painting by very gently rubbing the surface with a piece of white bread.

DOORS AND HARDWARE NEED A GOOD WIPE-DOWN

Doors with smooth, painted surfaces just need to be wiped down with a dry dusting cloth or a damp washcloth plus a little dishwashing liquid. Always work from the top down and regularly rinse the cloth to avoid wiping dirt back onto the door. For stained wood doors, wring out the cloth thoroughly so it's only just damp.

DECORATIVE DOOR ADVICE

Decorative features on a door can be tricky to clean as they often have tight corners that are hard to access with a cleaning cloth. An old toothbrush dampened with cleaning water is a handy tool—or even a toothpick for really tight spaces.

USE A DUST COVER

If you don't have a suitable space for a display cabinet, you can simply place a transparent cover over individual pieces that are particularly susceptible to gathering dust, such as model ships. An inexpensive plastic fish tank works well.

MAKE DUST COVERS

Keep dust and dirt out of a small appliance, power tool or keyboard. Cut the flaps off a cardboard box that will fit over the item, decorate it or cover it with self-adhesive contact paper, and use it as a dust cover.

Take Care

Stop dust before it starts. Your precious, fragile items are best kept in a glassed display cabinet to protect them from dust.

FEATHER DUSTERS WORK BEST FOR CHANDELIERS

Anyone with a chandelier in their home will take great pleasure in the magnificent light it produces, but they will also have their work cut out keeping it clean. At the installation stage, you should ensure that the chandelier can be lowered for easy cleaning. A feather duster is the best tool for the job; use it regularly to keep the crystals sparkling. If the cut glass pieces become dull over time, remove them individually and wash them in the sink as you would any other glassware. The same applies to acrylic chandeliers.

Handy Hack

The next time you climb high to clean a chandelier or ceiling fan, bring an old umbrella with you. Open the umbrella and hook its handle onto the fixture so that it hangs upside down to catch any drips or dust.

CHOOSING A FEATHER DUSTER

Ostrich feathers have barbs on them that catch and hold dust. Chicken feathers do not and make a poor duster. When using a duster, make smooth, controlled motions; don't wave it around like a pompom. Occasionally tap it on your ankle to release the dust onto the carpet where it can be vacuumed up.

FIND LOST TRINKETS

Have you ever tried searching through a carpet for a lost gemstone, contact lens or some other tiny, precious item? Try this solution: Cut a leg off an old pair of pantyhose with the toe section intact, and cover the nozzle of your vacuum cleaner with it. Secure the stocking in place with a tightly wound rubber band. Turn on the vacuum, carefully move the nozzle over the carpet and you'll soon find your lost valuable attached to the homemade filter.

FURNITURE FIXES

BEATING UPHOLSTERED ITEMS

Before beating large, upholstered furniture, cover it with a damp cloth to catch the dust being released. If you moisten the cloth with vinegar and water, the colors will look fresher afterward.

SAGGING SPOTS

If chairs have sagged or sofas have indentations where people have been sitting, moisten these pressure points with a little hot water, cover with white paper and iron dry. Just be careful not to burn these spots.

SWITCH IT UP!

Rearrange your furniture from time to time, or at least switch around the

Take Special Care with Leather

Maintain the beauty of your leather furniture for many years to come.

Scuff marks Restore the shine to scuffed leather upholstery by treating it with a mixture of equal parts beaten egg white and linseed oil.

Lost luster Has your leather couch or easy chair lost its luster? To restore it to its former glory, mix equal parts white vinegar and boiled linseed oil in a repurposed spray bottle, shake it up well, and spray it on. Spread it evenly over your furniture using a soft cloth, give it a couple of minutes to settle in and rub it off with a clean cloth.

Colorfast leather To treat older grease stains on colorfast leather, dip a cloth into hot water, wring it out, sprinkle on a small amount of baking soda and carefully rub the grease from the edge toward the middle. Go over it with a warm, moist cloth.

Ink stains Pour a little milk on a clean cloth and dab it on leather to help remove marks from a ballpoint pen.

Full-grain leather Use an eraser to remove grease stains on full-grain leather. But don't rub for too long or you risk damaging the leather. Remove water stains by allowing them to dry, then roughen them with a brush.

loose cushions. Most of us have a favorite place to sit, and the upholstery in these spots gets dirtier more quickly. Switching things around reduces the degree of uneven soiling.

Take Care Upholstery is easy to damage, so always check the solution you're using in an inconspicuous place first for color fastness. Some fabrics, especially rayon and viscose, water spot very easily. Leave these to a professional.

Smooth Surfaces

Keep it clean and staying smooth with this helpful advice.

Use a soap and water solution with a dash of vinegar to clean furniture with plastic tops.

If the glass panes of bookcases or display cases are very dirty, moisten a cotton ball with rubbing alcohol and rub the glass in circles to avoid streaking.

Marble should never be cleaned aggressively. Wipe it with a soft cloth moistened with 1 tablespoon (15 ml) liquid soap in 1 quart (1 L) water. Apply a mixture of 3 tablespoons (45 ml) baking soda and 1 quart (1 L) warm water to dull marble. Leave it for 15 minutes, rinse and rub dry.

DIRTY CUSHION SOLUTION

Clean dirty sofa cushions every year with a solution made from 1 part vinegar and 1 part water. Apply it with a cloth and wipe it off with tap water.

WASHING CUSHION COVERS

After washing cushion covers, iron them from the inside and put them back on the cushions while still damp; they will stretch better and dry without wrinkling.

WORKING WITH DARK VELVET

Clean dark velvet upholstery covers with a brush moistened in cold coffee. Then moisten a cloth with tap water and pat the velvet to pick up any excess.

Handy Hack

Rub soiled spots gently on wool or linen upholstery covers with a soft rubber eraser.

SOILED SYNTHETIC MATERIALS

Clean synthetic covers by dipping a cloth dampened with water in a little baking soda and gently rubbing the cushion with it. Go over it again with a water-and-soap solution. Test this on the reverse side first (or a corner) to make sure that it doesn't leave a mark.

Take Care How can you tell if the baking soda you've had stashed away in the back of your pantry is still fresh and safe to use? Just pour out a small amount—a little less than a teaspoon (5 ml)—and add a few drops of vinegar or fresh lemon juice. If it doesn't fizz, it's time to replace it with a new box. By the way, a sealed box of baking soda has an average shelf life of 18 months, while an opened box lasts 6 months.

WATER ON FABRIC UPHOLSTERY

After using water on fabric upholstery, cover the area with paper towels, weight them down and let them dry overnight.

GOT MILK SPOTS?

Treat milk spots immediately with cold water or a lather of moisturizing soap and lukewarm water. To finish, pat dry.

SHINE TABLETOPS

Wipe tabletops with lemon juice, drying them with paper towels before polishing with newspaper to keep them shining.

CLEAN UP OILY FURNITURE

Did you get a little too enthusiastic when spritzing the side tables with lemon oil? Don't live with that sticky feeling. Sprinkle cornstarch over the surface and leave it for a few minutes to absorb the excess. Wipe up the cornstarch, then buff to a shine with a soft, lint-free cloth.

HIDE A DENT

Small dents in inconspicuous locations on furniture can be filled with candle wax. Choose a candle to match the color of your furniture—but be aware that some colored candles are white in the middle. Light the candle and allow wax to drip into the dent. Beeswax, which can also be melted in a small pot, is good for light-colored wood. Give the wax a minute or two to cool down and begin to solidify,

then press it in firmly with your finger
and smooth down the surface.

TAKE CRAYON OFF
POLISHED WOOD

Did the kids color way outside the lines
on your varnished maple dining table?
No problem—but don't scrub it with
water or anything scratchy or you'll mar
the surface. Just rub on 1 to 2 tablespoons
(15 to 30 ml) of mayo with a paper towel
and let it sit. Rub again and, presto, the
marks are gone. Don't let your children
know how easy it is to repair that mistake
or they may try it again.

INSTANT FIX FOR
SCRATCHED WOODWORK

Your guests will be walking through
the door any minute when you happen
to notice several fresh, light scratches
on your dark-wood wall unit. What can
you possibly do on such short notice?
Rush to the kitchen, fetch a small cup
or container, and mix 1 teaspoon (5 ml)
instant coffee in 1 tablespoon (15 ml)
vegetable oil or water. Apply the mixture
with a cotton ball and let it dry. (This is
not recommended for valuable antiques
or shellac finishes.)

OIL STAIN ON WOOD

Grease from your hands or oil can leave

stains on untreated or dulled wood, as the
wood will absorb it. Press a cheesecloth
on it, then apply a warm iron to help
loosen and absorb the stain.

NO MORE WATER MARKS

Rub water stains on wood with a
mixture of equal parts white toothpaste
and baking soda. For light-colored
wood, try rubbing a Brazil nut over the
spot. For dark wood, dab a mixture of
wood ash and vegetable oil on the stains
using a cork.

GET RID OF WATER RINGS

To remove white rings left by wet glasses
on wooden furniture, mix equal parts
vinegar and olive oil and apply the
mixture with a soft cloth while moving
with the wood grain. Use another clean,

Rattan and Wicker Furniture

Attractive in many settings, follow some tips to make these pieces look their best.

Clean untreated cane, rattan or bamboo by vacuuming the furniture, then cleaning with a cloth dipped in a mild soap solution. For varnished wicker, cane or chairs with raffia or straw seats, soap and water should do the trick. A small, stiff brush is good for cracks.

Increase the durability of rattan or wicker by brushing it once a year with salt water.

Lighten the color of wicker by rubbing it with half a lemon or a mixture of salt and vinegar. Rinse thoroughly after treatment and dry naturally.

Get sagging wicker seats back into shape by dampening them with hot water and letting them dry outdoors for at least 24 hours. As the fibers dry, they tighten and shrink back to their original shape. Make sure they dry in the shade, as direct sunlight could bleach them.

Treat the underside of wicker furniture with lemon oil to keep it from drying out.

soft cloth to shine it up. To get white water rings off leather furniture, dab them with a sponge soaked in full-strength white vinegar.

REMOVE WHITE MARKS ON WOOD
Remove those white marks—caused by hot cups or sweating glasses—on your coffee table or other wooden furniture

by making a paste of 1 tablespoon (15 ml) baking soda and 1 teaspoon (5 ml) water. Gently rub the spot in a circular motion until it disappears. Remember, don't use too much water.

WAX ON WOODEN FURNITURE

Melt wax on wood with a blow-dryer on its slowest, hottest setting. Remove the softened wax with a paper towel (a plastic scraper can be useful here), then wipe the area with a cloth dipped in equal parts vinegar and water. Repeat if necessary. To remove wax from silver candlestick holders, use a blow-dryer to soften the wax, then just peel it off.

Handy Hack

Do you have some beer that's old or gone flat? Use it to clean wooden furniture. Just wipe it on with a soft cloth and off with another dry cloth.

WIPE OFF BUILDUP

When furniture polish or wax builds up on wood furniture or leather tabletops, get rid of it with diluted white vinegar. For wood furniture, dip a cloth in equal parts vinegar and water and squeeze it out well. Then, moving with the grain, clean away the polish. Wipe dry with a soft towel or cloth. For leather tabletops, simply wipe them down with a soft cloth dipped in ¼ cup (60 ml) vinegar and ½ cup (125 ml) water. Use a clean towel to dry off any remaining liquid.

HANDLE LAMPSHADES WITH CARE

Ideally, lampshades made of delicate fabric or paper should be cleaned with a fine brush. Stitched fabric shades can also be soaked carefully in the bathtub with warm water and a little dishwashing liquid. Rinse with clean water and then dry the shade carefully—start by soaking up water with paper towel and finish with a hair dryer. Work quickly and ensure that the shade is dried completely to prevent the metal frame from rusting.

BEDDING, A CLOSE COMFORT

For the sake of good hygiene, refrain from making the bed as soon as you get up. Allow the bedding to cool down and air out for a little while—with the window open if possible. This will allow much of the moisture the bedding has absorbed during your night's sleep to dissipate.

MATTRESS CLEANSE

A mattress must be aired and cleaned regularly. Take it out of the bedroom and let it breathe. Then, place a damp sheet on the mattress and beat it. A vacuum upholstery tool can also help.

NATURAL POLISHES

DIY LEMON OIL FURNITURE POLISH

Shine up your wood furniture, paneling and knickknacks with this natural polish that will take you only a minute to prepare and costs very little. Discard any leftovers and make up a fresh batch each time you want to polish your wood treasures.

- 1 cup (250 ml) olive oil
- ⅓ cup (80 ml) lemon juice
- 1 clean 16-oz. (500 ml) repurposed spray bottle

Combine the oil and lemon juice in the spray bottle. Shake well before using.

Apply a small amount of the mixture to a soft flannel cloth or chamois and apply it evenly over the wood surface.

Use a clean, dry flannel cloth to buff and polish.

RECIPE: NO-FUSS FURNITURE POLISH

How would you like a furniture polish that you can just wipe on and forget? This is the recipe for you—and for less than you'd expect!

- ¼ cup (60 ml) boiled linseed oil
- ⅛ cup (30 ml) vinegar
- ⅛ cup (30 ml) whiskey
- 1 clean 16-oz. (500 ml) repurposed spray bottle

Combine all the ingredients in the bottle. Shake well.

Apply a small amount of polish to a clean, soft cloth and wipe on. No need to buff; the dullness evaporates along with the alcohol.

MEDITERRANEAN POLISH

Most modern furniture sprays and polishes are nothing but silicone, which leaves a quick shine but builds up to a sticky dullness over time. For a much more environmentally friendly polish for finished wood surfaces, simply wipe on a dab of pure olive oil with a soft cloth, then buff to a shine.

 Take Care If your furniture has a polyurethane finish, the use of polish is inappropriate. You are merely spreading oil on plastic. If lacquered, it needs polishing only a few times per year. If it is oiled, it may need polishing more often. Always use the same polish each time. Many polishes and oils don't play well together.

ANTIQUE WOOD FURNISHINGS

Never expose antique wood to direct sun or treat with conventional polishes. Because of its age, it's delicate. Rather than using oils that can degrade the finish, polish antique furnishings with beeswax granules (available from a hardware store) made to treat antique wood for long-lasting protection.

TEAK OR ROSEWOOD FURNITURE

Shine teak or rosewood furniture with a mix of 1¼ cups (310 ml) beer, 1 tablespoon (15 ml) melted beeswax granules and 2 teaspoons (10 ml) sugar. Brush on thinly, let dry and buff with a cotton cloth.

TREAT WOOD VENEER

Bring out the shine of a fine wood veneer. Pour 1 cup (250 ml) olive oil and 4 teaspoons (20 ml) filtered fresh lemon juice in a glass bottle. Seal the bottle with a cork and shake vigorously for a minute. Open and apply the mixture to a 100% pure cotton ball, cover with a linen cloth or dish towel, and polish the veneer using a circular motion. Dry with a clean cloth.

WORKING WITH WALNUT

Bring out the grain and color of walnut by rubbing it with milk. Rubbing scratches with a walnut cut in half works well.

 Handy Hack Polish away small scratches on glass surfaces by smearing on a little toothpaste, then buffing it off with a soft cloth.

CLEAN TARNISHED BRASS

Say goodbye to tarnish on brass, copper or stainless steel. Make a paste of lemon juice and salt (or substitute baking soda

QUICK SILVER SHINE

Want a really easy, inexpensive and amazingly effective way to polish your silver without any smelly chemicals or commercial products? This is easier than using a silver dipping cleaner.

- 4 cups (1 L) hot water
- 3 tsp. (15 ml) baking soda or washing soda
- 3 tsp. (15 ml) salt
- 1 sheet aluminum foil

Fill the kitchen sink with about 4 cups (1 L) hot water.

Dissolve the baking soda or washing soda and salt in the water, then place the sheet of aluminum foil at the bottom of the sink.

Rest the tarnished silver on the foil for 10 seconds. Remove and dry with a soft flannel cloth.

KETCHUP COPPER POLISH

It can be a bit messy, but it works like a charm on unlacquered copper—and it's nontoxic.

- ½ to 1 cup (125 to 250 ml) tomato ketchup
- ¼ to 1 lemon, juiced

In a small bowl, combine the ketchup and lemon juice and stir to mix. How much you need of each ingredient depends on the size of the object you want to polish, but keep the ratio of ketchup to lemon juice about 8:1.

Spread out some old newspapers. Rub the mixture over the copper piece's surface. Let it sit for 5 to 10 minutes.

Thoroughly rinse the copper piece in warm water and dry with soft, clean cloths. Buff to a shine with a soft cloth.

or cream of tartar for the salt) and coat the affected area. Leave it on for about 5 minutes. Wash in warm water, rinse

and polish dry. Use the same mixture to clean metal kitchen sinks. Apply the paste, scrub gently and rinse.

REFRESH THOSE WALLS

BOTTOM TO TOP

As an exception to the usual top-down rule, when cleaning walls you should work from the bottom up, because any water drips will be easier to remove from a clean wall surface. Nevertheless, be sure to wipe these drips away as soon as they occur so they don't become permanent marks.

Take Care Be especially careful with water around electrical switches and power points. The plastic covers over switches and outlets can be wiped with a well wrung-out cloth, but make sure water doesn't penetrate inside.

ONE WALL AT A TIME

Always clean the entire surface of a wall in one go without taking a break. Otherwise you can end up with unsightly edge marks.

Take Care Never wet-wash your whitewashed walls as it will take the color off of them.

ERASE A QUESTIONABLE STAIN

If you find unidentifiable small smudges and spots on your walls, get rid of them with an art gum eraser. Rub the wall gently, and watch the stain disappear. You can also use an art gum eraser to rub fingerprints off wallpaper.

SIMPLE SPOT SOLUTION

Moisten spots and stains on a wall with a solution of water and dishwashing liquid. Wait for the mark to dissolve, then blot it up with a microfiber cloth. Do not rub!

RANDOM BALLPOINT-PEN MARKS?

Don't lose your cool. Instead, dab some full-strength white vinegar on the areas using a cloth or a sponge. Repeat until the marks are gone.

Handy Hack Remove your young Picasso's kitchen wall pencil sketches with a slice of fresh rye bread (seeded or not). Then go out and buy your child a nice big sketch pad.

USE BREAD ON WALLPAPER

Cut the crusts off a slice of white bread

and roll it up into a ball. Once the bread starts to feel slightly doughy, roll it over the bad spots on the wallpaper to lift off dirt or fingerprints. Test the bread ball first on an inconspicuous corner.

GET RID OF CRAYON MARKS

Has a small child redecorated your walls or wallpaper with some original artworks in crayon? Just grab a damp rag, dip it in some baking soda and lightly scrub the marks. They should come off with a minimum of effort. You can also try a clean, new piece of unsoaped steel wool and scrub the crayon lightly in one direction. You have a good chance of returning the wall to its pristine state.

WASH WALLPAPER

Wallpaper that's starting to look a bit dingy can be brightened up by wiping it with a rag or sponge moistened in a solution of 2 tablespoons (30 ml) baking soda in 4 cups (1 L) of water. To remove grease stains from wallpaper, make a paste of 1 tablespoon (15 ml) baking soda and 1 teaspoon (5 ml) water. Rub it on the stain, let it sit for 5 to 10 minutes and rub off with a damp sponge.

WATERPROOF WALLPAPER GRIME

If your kitchen walls are covered with waterproof wallpaper, remove excess dirt with a vacuum cleaner, then wash the walls with a solution of ½ cup (125 ml) lemon juice, ½ cup (125 ml) dishwashing liquid and 1 quart (1 L) water. Before starting, wash a tiny section in an out-of-sight place to make sure the paper will tolerate the mixture.

Take Care Never soak fabric or cork wallpaper, as either one will swell. Instead, carefully wipe the surface with a damp cloth. If too much water is applied, pat dry with a clean cloth. Carefully vacuum textured wallpaper on low power and avoid wet-washing it.

Dust Painted Walls and Wallpaper

Airborne dust particles can land on the tiniest imperfections in painted or wallpapered surfaces. If you run your hand over a wall that appears to be clean and find that your fingers are picking up dust, it's time to take action.

Start by running a dry microfiber dusting mop over the wall. Leave it at that for delicate surfaces such as fabric wallpapers.

For painted walls, if it's absolutely necessary you can wipe them down with a damp cloth. Just add a dash of dishwashing liquid to the cleaning water. Never use harsh chemicals or abrasive products, and avoid rubbing excessively. All of these can cause discoloration and leave ugly marks on the wall.

EASY WALLPAPER REMOVAL

You don't have to rent a commercial steamer or use toxic chemicals to strip your old wall covering. Here's an easy method that not only is nontoxic but is surprisingly inexpensive, too. Use a garden sprayer or a paint roller to apply a solution of equal parts white vinegar and hot water. Saturate an area of wallpaper, wait 10 minutes, then peel it off. If it is stubborn, try carefully scoring the wallpaper with the scraper before you spray on the vinegar solution. For extensive jobs, work with windows open; vinegar is nontoxic but has a strong odor.

Take Care Do not wet-wash brick walls—the moisture will soak into the porous masonry and could cause mildew or other damage.

REVITALIZE WOOD PANELING

Does the wood paneling in your study look dull and dreary? Liven it up with this simple homemade remedy. Mix together 2 cups (500 ml) warm water, 4 tablespoons (60 ml) white or apple cider vinegar and 2 tablespoons (30 ml) olive oil in a container, give it a couple of good shakes, and apply to wood with a clean cloth. Let the mixture soak in for several minutes, then polish with a dry cloth.

Take Care Wipe sealed, painted or varnished paneling with soapy water. Avoid using an abrasive powder that could leave scratches.

SPARKLING WINDOWS

SECRET INGREDIENT

Add a squirt of glycerin to the water to help windows resist dust year-round and reduce fogging in winter.

ONIONS FOR THE WIN

Add half a raw onion to wash water for gleaming windows. Onion eliminates grease stains because its sulfides are powerful cleaners.

Take Care Avoid washing windows in sunshine as the water dries too quickly and causes streaking. The sun also makes it hard to see if glass is clean. Extremely cold days aren't ideal either, because the glass is likely to be brittle. If you must wash windows in cold weather, add a dash or two of rubbing alcohol to the wash water. Overcast days are best for window cleaning.

BLACK TEA WORKS ON GLASS

Remove specks from glass panes with a clean cloth moistened in warm black tea. A couple of squirts of rubbing alcohol will also dissolve them, making it quick and easy to wipe them off.

EFFERVESCENT WASHER

One of the simplest and most effective glass window cleaners around is club soda, which dries without streaking. Just pour it into a repurposed spray bottle and spritz the windows, then dry with a cloth.

 Insider Tip When squeegeeing windows, moisten the edge of the squeegee to keep it from squeaking and also to improve contact with the window glass.

CLEAN AND POLISH

If you're like most people, you probably use a lot of paper towels for drying off your freshly washed windows. Did you know that crumpled-up newspaper dries and polishes windows even better than paper towels? And it's a lot cheaper, too. Do be careful, though, of ink coming off newspaper onto your hands and what you then touch with them. Or, use an old pair of tights to bring out the shine instead.

SHINING AND FROST-FREE!

Do your windows frost up during winter? Wash them with a solution of ½ cup (125 ml) rubbing alcohol to 1 quart (1 L) water to prevent frost. Polish the windows after you wash them to make them shine.

WINDOWSILL CLEANUP

Remove water stains on windowsills with a soft cloth moistened with a

Top Tips for Window Frames

These specific features—perhaps not often thought of—need cleaning attention too!

Vacuum the window frame joint with the appropriate nozzle on the vacuum cleaner before starting to clean with liquid.

Stick with hot, soapy water for washing aluminum or plastic frames. Scouring powder will scratch them.

Wipe wood window frames treated with clear glaze or varnish with a damp cloth. Replace the water frequently; to get them extra clean, rub them with a solution of equal parts rubbing alcohol and tap water.

Clean wooden window frames with a barely wet cloth, then dry with a clean, soft cloth.

Rub off specks on wood frames using a rough cloth moistened with water. Another option is to clean them with a mixture of reduced-fat milk and cold water in equal proportions.

solution of equal parts rubbing alcohol and tap water.

SPECIALIZED WINDOWS

Clean small windowpanes (skylights, louver windows, fanlights) with a chamois only. Thoroughly wet the chamois in the wash water, squeeze it out gently and work from the edge toward the center of the glass. Immediately wipe the glass dry to prevent streaking.

GLASS GONE DULL?

Rub dulled windows or mirrors with olive or linseed oil to get their shine back. Leave the oil on for an hour, wipe dry with tissue paper and clean as you normally do.

STAINED GLASS ON PURPOSE

Modern stained glass is so strong that it can be cleaned as you would normal glass panes. Take greater care with old stained glass: Simply wipe it carefully with a damp cloth. If the old glass is actually painted, don't wash it at all or you risk removing the color. Instead, dust the panes with a soft brush.

CARE FOR FROSTED GLASS

Clean frosted glass with hot vinegar

DIY SUPER WINDOW AND GLASS CLEANER

Forget about all of those store-bought window cleaners. Your windows can get a professional shine for next to nothing. The alcohol in this formula helps prevent streaking.

- ⅓ **cup (80 ml) white vinegar**
- ¼ **cup (60 ml) rubbing alcohol**
- 3¼ **cups (810 ml) water**
- 1 **clean 32-oz. (1 L) repurposed spray bottle**
   Old newspapers

Mix the vinegar, alcohol and water in the spray bottle. Shake the bottle well before using.

Spray on a dirty windowpane or other glass surface.

Dry with crumpled newspaper.

water to give it a dull sheen and carefully wipe dry.

DELICATE ETCHED GLASS

Dust etched glass with a soft brush, and clean the textured side of the glass with a chamois. You can simply squeegee the smooth side.

CLEAN DIRT OFF BLINDS

Nobody wants to get into the job of cleaning window blinds, but now and then the grime and dust is too much and you have to give it a go. Make your life simpler by using socks (or cloth garden gloves) and vinegar. Mix half and half water and vinegar, and draw a clean cotton tube sock loosely onto each hand. Dip the socks in the vinegar mixture and pull your hands along individual blinds, clutching top and bottom. The dirt will slip right off onto the socks. Dip them in clean water to rinse the dirt and back in the vinegar mix again for the next slat.

DUST-FREE VENETIAN BLINDS

Rubbing alcohol does a terrific job of cleaning the slats of venetian blinds. Wrap a flat tool—a spatula or a 6-inch (15 cm) cement trowel—in cloth and secure with a rubber band, dip into some rubbing alcohol, and go to work.

Long-Lasting Chamois

Do yourself a favor: Buy a real chamois. It absorbs water more quickly and is easily squeezed out. With proper care it will last for years.

Keep your chamois soft and smooth by using it only with water or solutions made with water and vinegar or alcohol. Detergents will remove the leather's oils and leave it stiff.

Rinse out a chamois with warm salt water after every use to keep it soft.

Never wring a chamois. Instead, squeeze it gently, open it up, shake it out and let it dry slowly in the air.

FLOORS, CARPETS AND RUGS

DOUBLE UP ON WELCOME MATS

A nice welcome mat gives guests a place to wipe their feet—but a second mat inside the door will catch a lot of the dirt they knocked loose outside. Be sure to shake the dirt off welcome mats from time to time; otherwise, you're just giving your guests a place to pick up debris to track around your house!

CONSIDER A SHOES-OFF POLICY

Getting into the habit of removing shoes at the door will keep your family and visitors from tracking dirt into the house. Keep woolly socks for each family member or a pair of slippers for visitors to wear near the door, so everyone can change from outdoor to indoor footwear.

USE CARE WHEN WASHING WOOD

If your floor still looks dirty after sweeping or vacuuming, you will need to wash it as well. Avoid cleaning the floor with an excessive amount of water as this can leave marks or even cause the wood to swell. Wring out your mop thoroughly so it is only just damp. Use of a microfiber flat mop can help control moisture.

Take Care

Using a damp mop with a mild vinegar solution is a common way to clean wooden and wax-free vinyl or laminate flooring. But, if at all possible, check with your flooring manufacturer first as it may void your warranty. Even when diluted, vinegar's acidity can ruin some floor finishes, and too much water will damage most wooden floors. Never use vinegar on marble surfaces, and make sure it's properly diluted before using it on grout or it may eat it away.

GOING WITH VINEGAR

If you want to try vinegar on your floors, after checking with the manufacturer, use ½ cup (125 ml) white vinegar mixed in a gallon (4 L) warm water. Use a trial application in an inconspicuous area. Before applying the solution, squeeze out the mop thoroughly (or just use a spray bottle to moisten the mop head directly).

Handy Hack

You can add a dash of olive oil to the cleaning water to prevent static from building up.

COTTON SQUARES FOR MOPPING

Those household mops and sweepers with disposable wipes fitted to the mop head seem like a great idea until you realize you have to buy replacement cloths over and over and over—they get expensive quickly and aren't very environmentally friendly. Instead, cut absorbent cotton scraps into a suitable size replacement and use real fabric instead of those pricey store-bought replacements. For wet mops, use a rectangular strip of terry cloth or toweling.

 Insider Tip If you mop the floor in the same direction as the boards are laid, you will reduce the appearance of streaks or lines.

DUST OFF YOUR MOPS

Dust mops make it a breeze to get the dust bunnies and pet hair around your home, but how do you get the stuff off the mop? Place a large paper bag over the mop head and use a piece of string or a rubber band to keep it from slipping off. Now give it several good shakes (a few gentle bumps wouldn't hurt either). Lay the mop on its side for a few minutes to let the dust in the bag settle. Then carefully remove the bag for easy disposal of dusty dirt.

GIVE BROOMS A LONGER LIFE

A new straw broom will last longer if you soak its bristles in a bucket of hot, salty water. After about 20 minutes, remove the broom and let it dry.

UNSIGHTLY MARKS

When children choose to express their artistic talents on the floor before you can intervene, the pencil or wax crayon marks they leave behind are a particular cleaning challenge. You can remove pencil marks with a kneadable artist's eraser that won't leave behind colored marks. For wax crayon marks, place an ice pack or cold compress from the freezer over the area; scratch the marks away carefully with a plastic spatula (the kind designed for nonstick pans) or use your fingernail.

SWEEP WITH TEA

Some rural Japanese housekeepers traditionally strewed still-damp tea leaves over the floor before sweeping—and some no doubt still do. Dust and dirt cling to the leaves and are easier to push into a dustpan. You can then throw the contents into a garden bed or compost pile. (Talk about an eco-friendly cleanser!) Just don't use tea leaves on unbleached wood or carpeting, since tea may stain.

AN IRON TO THE RESCUE

If you accidentally dripped candle wax onto your wood floor, you need to remove the stain pronto. How? Place an ordinary brown paper bag over the offending mark,

and run a warm iron over the bag until it soaks up the stain. The same strategy will work to remove wax stains on carpet, as long as you scrape off as much wax as possible before you start.

PEP-IT-UP FLOOR WASH

Make a peppermint tea floor-cleaning solution that's good and strong!

1	qt. (1 L) water
6	peppermint tea bags
1	qt. (1 L) white vinegar
2	Tbsp. (30 ml) baby oil
1	tsp. (5 ml) dishwashing liquid

In a large saucepan, boil 1 quart (1 L) water, remove from heat, and add peppermint tea bags. Let steep 2 hours.

Pour tea into a mop pail and add vinegar, baby oil and dishwashing liquid. Stir with a large kitchen spoon to mix.

Dip a clean mop into the solution, wring or squeeze it out, and mop away.

MARBLE OR GRANITE FLOORS

All a marble or granite floor needs is to be swept or vacuumed and cleaned with a microfiber or sponge mop. You can use either a little water or a lot—the surface isn't sensitive to moisture. You won't go wrong using just plain old water, and this will also prevent soap streaks. In hard-water areas, to avoid mineral deposits from appearing, dry the floor thoroughly with a cloth or use deionized water available from hardware stores.

Take Care Don't use vinegar—or alcohol or lemon juice—on marble tabletops, countertops or floors. Vinegar's acidity can dull or even pit the protective coating—and possibly damage the stone itself. Also, avoid using vinegar on travertine and limestone; the acid eats through the calcium in the stonework.

SAWDUST FOR STONE

Expensive stone-floor cleaning products sold in hardware stores are not always necessary to get the job done. Try wetting the floor with a well-wrung mop, sprinkle it with sawdust (try your local hardware store), then give it a good scrub with a stiff brush. When you're done, sweep up the sawdust then vacuum to catch the rest.

MILK AND LINOLEUM

You don't have to use a costly cleaning product specifically made for linoleum flooring. Use a mixture of equal parts water and milk to give a linoleum floor a fresh shine.

Take Care Avoid using abrasive cleansers on linoleum, whether powders or creams. These can dull the surface and it will get dirty again more quickly. Also avoid using cleaners with strong solvents or high or low pH.

WASH AWAY CARPET GLUE

Removed your carpet only to find old glue stuck to the subfloor? Don't scrape it off; instead, mix a solution of 3 parts hot water and 1 part vinegar. Spread the mixture over the subfloor and let sit for 30 minutes. The softened glue will come right off with a putty knife.

VACUUMING CARPET

Whenever possible, run the vacuum in the same direction as the carpet's weave, as this is more gentle on the carpet. Occasionally, you will need to vacuum against the weave to loosen dirt out of the deeper pile, but smooth the carpet down again after doing so.

IMPRINTS BY FURNITURE

Remove furniture imprints on rugs by placing a damp cloth on the spot and ironing it carefully. Then brush the fibers in the opposite direction. You could also place an ice cube on the compressed fibers to make them swell up and then vacuum to make the pile stand up again.

Take Care

Never use harsh cleaning products on carpet. Try water first—deionized water is best—or sparkling mineral water or club soda. Don't scrub, especially cut pile. It can untwist fibers and then you'll need a new carpet piece!

Magic for Carpet Stains

You can lift many stains from your carpet with vinegar.

Rub light carpet stains with 2 tablespoons (30 ml) salt dissolved in ½ cup (125 ml) white vinegar. Let dry and vacuum.

For larger or darker stains, add 2 tablespoons (30 ml) borax to the mixture and use it in the same way.

For tough, ground-in dirt and stains, make a paste of 1 tablespoon (15 ml) vinegar with 1 tablespoon (15 ml) cornstarch and rub into the stain using a dry cloth. Let it sit for two days and then vacuum.

Take Care Never put salt on fresh red wine spills because it will set the stain and could leave an indelible blue mark on the pile. Also, it will cause the carpet to remain damp.

GET INK OUT

Oh no, ink on the carpet! In this case a little spilled milk might save you from crying. Mix the milk with cornstarch to make a paste. Apply the paste to the ink stain. Allow the concoction to dry on the carpet for a few hours, brush off the dried residue and vacuum it up.

COFFEE OR TEA SPILL?

Choose one of these two methods and act fast to remove a coffee or tea stain from carpet. Pour club soda liberally onto the stain and blot, repeating as necessary. Or beat an egg yolk, rub it into the stain and blot it.

SIMPLE CHOCOLATE SOLUTION

Remove hardened chocolate on carpet with a knife, and dab away the residue with cold water, followed by warm water.

REMOVE WINE AND GREASE STAINS

It's bound to happen sometime. Someone drops a slab of butter or a glass of red wine on your beautiful white carpeting. Before you panic, get a paper towel and blot up as much of the stain as possible. Then sprinkle a liberal amount of baking soda over the spot. Give it at least an hour to absorb the stain and vacuum up the remaining powder.

GUM ON THE RUG

Horrified to find a big wad of chewing gum stuck to the rug? Don't worry. Place a plastic bag filled with ice cubes over it. This will make the chewing gum brittle and it can then be chipped away with a spatula or spoon.

FRUIT OR FRUIT JUICE SPLATTER

If you have a spill with fruit involved, first pick up any solid pieces of fruit on your carpet, then stir 1 tablespoon (15 ml) laundry detergent and 1½ tablespoons (23 ml) white vinegar into 2 cups (500 ml) water. Gently work the solution into the stain and then blot.

FRIED CHICKEN FAIL

Accidentally drop that family-size bucket of takeout fried chicken on the den carpet? Sprinkle the grease spots liberally with cornmeal or cornstarch, let sit for several hours, and vacuum it up. All better!

KETCHUP BEGONE

Jump right on this one, because once a ketchup stain sets on carpet, it won't come out (ever). Grab the salt and sprinkle it over the spill, let sit for a few minutes, and vacuum. Sponge up any residue and continue salting and vacuuming until the stain is completely gone.

Insider Tip Use cold mineral water on bloodstains on a rug, blotting with a clean towel as you go.

CLEAN UP PAINT SPILLS WITH VINEGAR

Spring into action before a paint stain sets into carpet: Mix 1½ teaspoons (7.5 ml) vinegar and 1½ teaspoons (7.5 ml) laundry detergent into 2 cups (500 ml) warm water. Now sponge away the paint (a task that takes time and elbow grease), and rinse with cold water. If you're lucky, what might have been an unwelcome (and permanent) decorating touch will be gone.

COLD CLEANSE FOR A RUG

Instead of going to the expense of hiring a machine to shampoo a rug, people who live in colder regions can take advantage of a heavy fall of fresh snow. Leave your rug outside for a few hours to get cold. Then lay it face down on an area of clean snow and give it a thorough beating. You will be amazed by the amount of dust

RECIPE: HERBAL CARPET FRESHENER

Many commercial air and carpet deodorizers simply mask odors. To truly freshen carpets around your home, try this inexpensive natural formula instead.

Large handful of fresh lavender flowers
1 cup (250 ml) baking soda

In a large bowl, crush the lavender flowers to release scent.

Add the baking soda and mix well. Pour the mixture into a cheese shaker or a can with holes punched in the lid.

Sprinkle liberally on the carpet. Wait 30 minutes, then vacuum.

RECIPE: SPICY CARPET FRESHENER

Add a nice smell to your rooms while you freshen the carpets with this simple mixture.

1 cup (250 ml) baking soda or cornstarch
7 to 10 drops essential oil in a favorite scent (eucalyptus or rosewood, for example)

In a large bowl, combine the baking soda or cornstarch with the essential oil. Break up any clumps with a fork and stir well. Pour the mixture into a cheese shaker or a can with holes punched in the lid.

Sprinkle liberally on the carpet. Wait 30 minutes, then vacuum.

that comes out and turns the white snow gray. Turn the carpet over, cover it with clean snow, then sweep off the snow thoroughly. Bring the carpet back inside, allow the surface to dry completely and then vacuum to separate out the fibers again.

RESTORE WORN RUGS

If your rugs or carpets are looking worn and dingy from too much foot traffic or an excess of kids' building blocks, toy trucks and such, bring them back to life by brushing them with a clean broom dipped in a solution of 1 cup (250 ml) white vinegar in a gallon (4 L) water.

Your faded threads will perk up, and you won't even need to rinse off the solution.

BEAT A RUG

Dust and dander collect daily on (and in) area rugs, so shake 'em out the old-fashioned way: Hang the rug over a rail or taut clothesline and beat it. Your beater? A tennis racket.

Handy Hack

Spray straw rugs occasionally with a little salt water to help keep them flexible.

GIVE CARPETS A FRESH SCENT

Before vacuuming a room, sprinkle a little cornstarch on your carpeting. Wait about half an hour and vacuum as usual. (Make sure to vacuum any powders thoroughly to prevent build up.)

RID A RUG OF A BAD SMELL

Use baking soda to remove bad smells from rugs. Simply sprinkle it on the surface, let it work for 30 minutes and vacuum it up. For stubborn odors, rub the carpet first with vinegar and water, then apply the baking soda.

DIY: Rug Cleaning Tips

Your rugs can look brand-new again. Just try one of these easy natural methods.

Use a homemade cleaning powder for rugs. To make, mix 3 tablespoons (45 ml) soap flakes with 2 cups (500 ml) cornstarch. Sprinkle it on the rug, work it in with a scrub brush and vacuum.

Clean and freshen a rug by sprinkling it with moist salt. Let the salt work for a few minutes and then vacuum.

Grate fresh potatoes and scald them with boiling water. After 3 hours, strain them and brush the rug with the potato water. Let it dry and then vacuum.

Freshen a rug's colors by rubbing it with vinegar and water.

UNPLEASANT ODORS

MAKE A SCENTED AIR FRESHENER

Buying fragranced air fresheners can get expensive. Here is a wonderful way to make your room smell like a rose any time of the year. Layer rose petals and salt in a pretty jar with a tight-fitting lid. Remove the lid to freshen the room.

SWEETEN THE HOUSE

People who are allergic to air fresheners and sprays can still enjoy the benefits of a sweet-smelling house. Wet a cotton ball with vanilla and dab it very lightly on the outside of a regular light bulb (not a halogen bulb) in lamps. When you turn on the lamp, the bulb heats up and a faint but alluring scent of vanilla drifts out.

DIY ROOM HUMIDIFIER

Freshen and moisturize the air in your home on dry winter days. Make your own room scent that also doubles as a humidifier. If you have a wood-burning stove, place an enameled cast-iron pot or bowl on top, fill with water, and add lemon (and/or orange) peels, cinnamon sticks, cloves and apple skins. If you don't have a wood-burning stove, use your stovetop instead and just simmer the water periodically.

NO MORE PAINT SMELL

The smell of fresh paint can hang around for quite some time. You can help get rid of it by placing two halves of a freshly cut onion in opposite corners of the room. Chemicals in the onion will help absorb the odor of latex paint, and in one or two days the smell will be completely gone.

Handy Hack Another trick to rid a room of paint fumes is to place a couple of shallow dishes filled with undiluted white vinegar around a freshly painted room.

LINGERING TOBACCO ODORS

To get rid of a tobacco smell, place

RECIPE: ROOM FRESHENER SPRAY

Why waste your money on commercial air fresheners when it's so easy to make your own favorite scents? Use this spray judiciously, however. A room should have a hint of the scent, not an overpowering perfume. You can combine up to three essential oils to create a fragrance that suits you. Other choices include eucalyptus, lavender, geranium, grapefruit, orange, peppermint, pine, juniper, rose and spearmint.

1	clean 12-oz. (375 ml) repurposed spray bottle
¼	cup (60 ml) rubbing alcohol
25	drops bergamot essential oil
8	drops clove essential oil
5	drops lemon essential oil
1	cup (250 ml) distilled water

In the spray bottle, combine the rubbing alcohol and the essential oils and shake well to disperse the oil. Add the distilled water and shake for a minute or two more to blend all the ingredients thoroughly.

Let the mixture sit for a few days before using to allow the fragrance to blend and mature. A quick spritz is all that's needed to freshen a room.

RECIPE: SPICY ROOM FRESHENER

This fragrant mixture makes you think an apple pie is in the oven. Real estate agents sometimes suggest putting this mixture on the stove before prospective buyers come to see a house.

3	cups (750 ml) water
6	cloves
1	cinnamon stick
6	pieces dried orange peel

In a small saucepan, combine all the ingredients and bring to a boil over medium heat. Reduce the heat and simmer, uncovered, until your home is filled with a fresh, spicy scent. (Don't let the water boil away.)

saucers of baking soda in a room. Close the door and let them work overnight. Sprinkling fabric with baking soda also works; shake it off outside or vacuum in the morning. Rinse ashtrays with a vinegar solution and sprinkle coffee grounds in them to help absorb the scent.

BYE-BYE COOKING SMELLS

Get rid of smoke or cooking odors quickly and effectively by wetting a cloth in vinegar and waving it around the room you're trying to air. Soon you'll be able to take a big sniff of nothing.

CONTAINERS AND LUGGAGE

Do you have a plastic container or wooden box with a persistent, unpleasant odor? Stuff in a few sheets of crumpled newspaper and seal it closed for three or four days. You can also use this technique to deodorize trunks and suitcases, using more newspaper, of course.

LITTLE SOMETHING FOR A CLOSET

A piece of soap or a small sachet of lavender, cedar chips or even coffee grounds will add fragrance to a closet. Also, try to hang coats and jackets outside to air before returning them to the closet.

REFRESH DRAWERS AND CLOSETS

Put baking soda sachets to work on persistent musty odors in dresser drawers, sideboards or closets. Just fill the toe of a clean sock or stocking with 3 to 4 tablespoons (45 to 60 ml) baking soda, put a knot about 1 inch (2.5 cm) above the bulge and either hang it up or place it away in an unobtrusive corner. Use a few sachets in large spaces like closets and attic storage areas. Replace them every other month if needed.

ICK, VACUUM STENCH!

If exhaust from the vacuum cleaner smells unpleasant, change the bag and vacuum up some lavender flowers or peppermint leaves. Or dab a cotton ball with a little perfume or aromatic oil and vacuum that up.

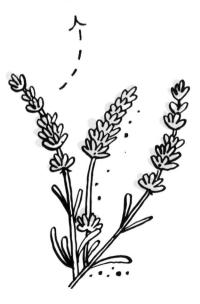

MUSTY ODOR FROM BOOKS

Place a musty book in a brown paper bag with 2 tablespoons (30 ml) baking soda. Don't shake the bag, just tie it up and let it sit in a dry place for about one week. When you open the bag, shake off remaining powder; no more smell!

GARBAGE CAN VS. BAKING SODA

Before you put a new liner in the garbage can, sprinkle in a dollop of baking soda. When you take out the full bag, turn the can upside down to dump any dry soda still left in there, and then add more before the new bag.

REDUCE FIREPLACE ODOR

There's nothing cozier on a cold winter night than a warm fire burning in the fireplace—but what if the fire smells horrible? Try throwing a few lemon peels into the flames. Or simply burn some lemon peels along with your firewood as a preventive measure.

Handy Hack

After removing ashes from the fireplace, set a plate of baking soda inside for a day to get rid of the sooty odor.

BAKING SODA

DE-STINK A BASEMENT

You don't have to live with that musty-smelling basement. Once you've taken care of the source of the moisture, combat any lingering odor by mixing 4 pounds (1.8 kg) kitty litter with 2 pounds (0.9 kg) baking soda in a large container. Then fill several coffee cans to the brim and place them around your basement. Replace with fresh mixture as needed.

Handy Hack

If your humidifier starts to smell awful, just pour 3 or 4 teaspoons (15 or 20 ml) lemon juice in the water. It not only will remove the bad odor but will replace it with a lemon-fresh fragrance. Repeat every couple of weeks to keep the odor from returning.

DEALING WITH MOLD

MOLD REMOVER FOR LEATHER

If you discover mold on leather, get at it with this simple removal recipe. Test on a small area first.

- ½ cup (125 ml) rubbing alcohol
- ¼ cup (60 ml) water
- 1 clean 8-oz. (250 ml) repurposed spray bottle

Combine ingredients in spray bottle and shake well to mix.

Spray affected area. Let the solution sit for 10 to 20 minutes, then wipe off mold with a clean rag and allow the item to thoroughly air-dry.

DIY SPOT MOLD AND MILDEW REMOVER

Mix up a batch of this powerful but benign-smelling cleaner to get rid of small patches of mold and mildew.

- ½ cup (125 ml) white vinegar
- 3 tsp. (15 ml) borax
- 2 cups (500 ml) hot water
- 1 clean 32-oz. (1 L) repurposed spray bottle

Combine ingredients in spray bottle. Shake well.

Spray on surfaces where mold or mildew is forming. Wipe off mold and mildew, but leave the cleaning solution residue to keep the problem from returning.

PUT CHALK IN YOUR CLOSET

Tie a dozen pieces of chalk together and hang them up in a damp closet. The chalk will absorb moisture and help prevent mold. Replace the chalk bundle with a new one every few months.

SPACE FOR TALL FURNITURE

If possible, leave a clearance of at least ¼ to ½ inch (0.6 to 1.3 cm) between armoires or bookcases and your home's outer walls. Mold can develop behind tall furniture.

SHOE SOLUTIONS

GET UNSTUCK

Stepped in gum? You could try scraping it off, but here's an easy way to remove it. Stick a small piece of paper over the gum and place the shoe in the freezer for 1 to 2 hours. Take the shoe out and peel the paper off. The gum should peel off with the paper! If any residue is left, a simple scrape with a knife should do the trick.

DON'T THROW OUT SMELLY SHOES

Not surprisingly, well-used sports shoes tend to become stinky. One simple remedy is to sprinkle a little baking soda into shoes, let it stand overnight, then vacuum it out in the morning. When you're not wearing your sneakers, stuff them with a pair of socks filled with cat litter to absorb the odor and any moisture. A final option is to place shoes in a zip-top bag in the freezer overnight to kill odor-causing bacteria.

A SAGE ANSWER

Crumble a bit of dried sage into each shoe before putting it on. Sage is not only gently fragrant, but it actually attacks the bacteria that make your teenager's gym shoes smell so bad. Shake out the flecks at night, and add a new leaf the next day.

Handy Hack

Cornstarch can also be an effective treatment for any smelly shoes. Sprinkle it on and leave overnight. Shake out shoes well the next day, then dry with a blow-dryer.

DEODORIZE CANVAS SHOES

Canvas shoes can get pretty smelly, especially if you wear them without socks in the summertime. Knock down the odor and soak up the moisture by occasionally sprinkling a little salt in your canvas shoes.

WINTERTIME SALT STAINS

Getting ice and snow on your shoes and boots is bad enough, but worse still is the rock salt that's used to melt it in some cold areas. In addition to leaving unsightly white stains, salt can actually cause footwear to crack and even disintegrate if it's left on indefinitely. To remove it and prevent long-term damage, wipe fresh stains with a cloth dipped in undiluted white vinegar.

WATER MARKS ON LEATHER

Water marks on smooth leather shoes are best removed by rubbing at the marks with the cut side of half an onion or a little lemon juice. Leave on briefly, then brush off. Remove water marks from suede leather by rubbing them off with salt.

Insider Tip

Are your suede shoes feeling blue? Are they dirty and stained? Cheer them up! By very gently scuffing with sandpaper, you can revive the nap and take off some stains.

THOSE LOVABLE RUBBER BOOTS

To clean rubber boots, simply mix up a solution of warm water and dishwashing liquid in a repurposed spray bottle. Spray on, leave for a few minutes, then buff off with an old rag.

WICK WATER FROM WET SHOES

To speed air-drying, stuff water-soaked shoes and boots with crumpled newspaper, which will wick out the moisture. Speed the drying even more by placing the shoes or boots on their sides, turning them over from time to time, and replacing the newspaper as it becomes damp.

GO BANANAS FOR THAT SHEEN

Using a banana peel is actually a great way to put the shine back on your silverware and leather shoes. First, remove any of the leftover stringy material from the inside of the peel, then just start rubbing the inside of the peel on your shoes or silver. When you're done, buff with a paper towel or soft cloth. You might even want to use this technique to restore your leather furniture. Test it on a small section first before you take on the whole piece.

SHINE THAT JEWELRY

DIY: Perk Up Your Bling

If your jewelry has become tarnished or dirty over time, despite your most careful storage efforts, there are a few simple home remedies to clean and restore it to its full glory.

Simply wipe fashion jewelry with a damp cloth, as detergents may damage the material. Sprinkle soiled jewelry with baking soda and gently scrub it with a soft toothbrush, then rinse with warm water and pat dry.

Place gold jewelry in a kitchen strainer for cleaning (clean pieces individually so they do not become scratched). Add a little dishwashing liquid and hold the strainer under running hot water. You can also clean solid gold jewelry (that is not merely gold-plated) with baking soda: First apply the powder to a damp cotton pad, wipe the piece carefully and then rinse.

Onion juice will perk up gold jewelry that has lost its shine; leave the juice on for about

3 hours, then polish it away with a soft cloth.

Clean tarnished sterling silver jewelry with aluminum foil: Cover a deep plate or bowl with foil, place the jewelry on top, sprinkle with salt, then pour boiling water over it. Let it stand for an hour, then polish the pieces with a soft cloth to restore their full shine. Alternatively,

cont. on p. 140

cont. from p. 139

wrap the jewelry in aluminum foil, place in a saucepan of water and briefly bring to a boil. Be careful, though: Don't use the foil method if silver jewelry has intentionally blackened parts that create an antique finish, as it will brighten these, too. Also avoid this method if your jewelry contains porous precious stones such as turquoise or pearls. A gentler alternative is to place the jewelry in a saucepan of water, add ½ teaspoon (2.5 ml) of dishwashing liquid and boil it for 2 to 3 minutes.

Gemstones must be treated with care. Use a fine brush to remove dust and clean hard gemstones such as diamonds, rubies and sapphires with pure alcohol. Remove soap, grease and cosmetics, which may accumulate in claw or prong settings, with a soft toothbrush, then rinse and pat dry with a microfiber cloth.

Take Care
Do not apply vinegar to items of jewelry containing pearls or gemstones because it can damage their finish or, in the case of pearls, actually disintegrate them. Also, do not attempt to remove tarnish from the surface of antiques, because it could diminish their value significantly.

GOLDEN BEER TRICK

Get the shine back in your solid gold rings (without gemstones) and other jewelry by pouring a bit of beer (not dark ale!) on a soft cloth and rubbing it gently over the piece. Use a clean second cloth or dish towel to dry it thoroughly.

PREVENT OXIDATION

Silver can oxidize (turn black) if it is not worn for extended periods. It is therefore best to wrap your silver rings, earrings, necklaces and bracelets in aluminum foil or a silver cleaning cloth. Another option is to keep a piece of chalk with your silver jewelry to prevent oxidation.

KEEP IT SPARKLING!

Use ketchup to polish your silver jewelry. If a ring or bracelet has a smooth surface, dunk it in a small bowl of ketchup for a few minutes. If it has a detailed surface, use a toothbrush and work the ketchup into the crevices. Don't leave ketchup on a piece any longer than necessary. Rinse and dry thoroughly.

FIZZING FOR PRECIOUS GEMS

Club soda gently and safely cleans precious jewels, whether it's your wedding diamond or your Great-Aunt Ruby's emerald. Put the jewels in a glass and top with club soda. Let them soak overnight. The fizzing bubbles will lift away dirt and grime that dull the gleam. Dry and polish gently with a soft cloth.

Caring for Amber and Pearls

Amber and pearl jewelry needs special care, as these nonmineral materials are more delicate than gemstones and most jewelry stones.

Clean soiled amber with lukewarm water and pat dry immediately. A few drops of olive oil buffed onto amber will restore shine. Spread white chalk on grease stains, leave on for a few hours and then wipe off with a soft cloth. Amber is affected by heat so it's best not to wear it while cooking. Also do not let amber air-dry when you clean it, as you risk turning the stone cloudy. Air-drying is fine for pearls.

The best care you can give pearls is to wear them often, as skin contact makes them retain their luster. However, remember to give them a wipe with a soft wool cloth after each wear. Periodically remove dust, sweat and grime by dabbing the pearls with a cloth dipped in a dilute solution of alcohol and water. Re-dip the cloth in fresh water to wipe clean, then buff dry with a soft cloth.

TIPS FOR ELECTRONICS

CLEAR DIRT OFF OFFICE GEAR

Your computer, printer and other home-office equipment will work better if you keep them clean and dust-free. Before you start cleaning, make sure that all your equipment is turned off. Now mix equal parts white vinegar and water in a bucket. Dampen a clean cloth in the solution—never use a spray bottle; you don't want to get liquid on the circuits inside—then squeeze it out as hard as you can so that it is only moist, and start wiping.

KEYBOARD CLEANING

It doesn't take long for a computer keyboard to get pretty dirty. First disconnect the keyboard from the computer, turn it upside down and give it a shake. Suck up any remaining dirt with a vacuum or blow it away with a hair dryer. To clean the keys, rub with a barely moist cotton swab dipped in baking soda. If your computer monitor is dusty, wipe it off with a clean, soft cloth.

Handy Hack

Keep a small, unused fine-bristle paintbrush at your desk and you can clean the keyboard when the impulse strikes. It's also great for getting rid of the gunk that collects in the hinges of a laptop. Another smart small tool to have around if you don't have a paintbrush? Cotton swabs. Keep a few of these helpers on hand for getting to the buildups in tight spaces on and near your computer and other electronics.

Take Care

Be aware to not clean keyboards or computer monitors with water. If the smallest drop gets inside, it can destroy your equipment.

Care for Your Flat-Screen TV

The surface of a flat-screen TV is made of a delicate plastic and should be cleaned using only a slightly dampened microfiber cloth. If the screen is really dirty, put a tiny drop of dishwashing liquid onto the cloth (not onto the screen directly!) and wipe carefully. Follow these other do's and don'ts when cleaning your TV:

DO turn the TV off first—so you don't interfere with the pixels and so that you can see the dirt more clearly.

DO use a soft cotton or microfiber cloth to clean all the crevices on the TV.

DON'T press hard: you can damage the screen.

DON'T use paper towel or rags: they are abrasive.

DON'T use window-cleaning fluid or any other chemical cleanser to clean the TV.

MOUSE TROUBLE?

If you have a mouse with a removable tracking ball, use a 50:50 vinegar–water solution to clean it. First, remove the ball from underneath the mouse by twisting the cover over it off. Use a cloth, dampened with the solution and wrung out, to wipe the ball clean and to remove fingerprints and dirt from the mouse itself. Then use a moistened cotton swab to clean out the gunk and debris from inside the ball chamber (let it dry for a couple of hours before reinserting the ball).

REMOTES SHOULD REMAIN DRY

Be gentle when cleaning a remote control. It's best to use a dry cloth only. Moisture must not be allowed to get inside.

A GOOD PHONE ROUTINE

Is your phone getting a bit grubby? Wipe it down with rubbing alcohol. It not only will remove the grime, but also will sanitize your phone at the same time.

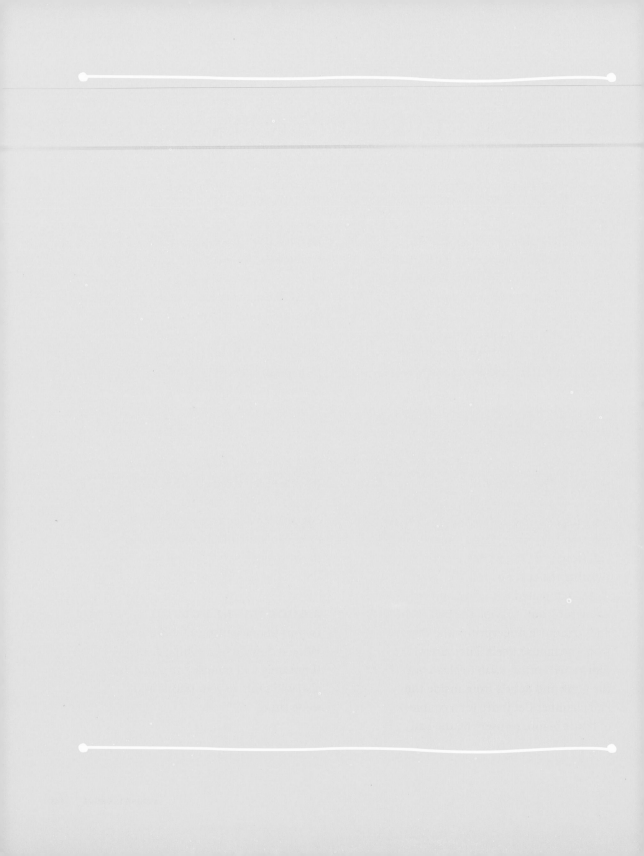

GARAGE AND CARS

IN THE GARAGE

CLEAN CONCRETE WITH KOOL-AID!

The same acids that make lemonade-flavored Kool-Aid taste good are a potent cleaning solution before you add water and sugar. Mix the contents of a package with 2 tablespoons hot water to make a paste, then rub that paste over rust stains in concrete. Scrub with a stiff cleaning brush and the stains will disappear. Rinse well.

MAKE A DRIP PAN FOR OIL LEAKS

Prevent an oil leak from soiling your garage floor or driveway by making a drip pan. All you need to do is to place a few sheets of corrugated cardboard on a cookie sheet or a shallow baking dish and place the pan under your car's drip. For better absorption, just sprinkle some cat litter, sawdust or oatmeal into the pan on top of the cardboard. Replace with fresh cardboard as needed.

WIPE THOSE LAWN MOWER BLADES

Grass, especially when it's damp, has a tendency to accumulate on your lawn mower blades after you cut the lawn—sometimes with grubs hiding inside.

Wipe down the blades with a cloth dampened with undiluted white vinegar. It will clean off leftover grass on the blades, as well as any pests that are stuck to the blades.

USE CHALK TO PREVENT RUST

Keep rust out of your toolbox—and stop your tools from pitting and rusting—by placing a few pieces of chalk in the toolbox. The chalk will absorb any moisture and keep the tools (and the toolbox) rust free.

The Dirt on Garage (and Basement) Floors

They're often the least thought-of floors in (and out of) the house, but garage and unfinished basement floors take a lot of hard knocks, daily. Never mind your car: If you store your lawn mower, leaf blower or string trimmer in this space, you're bound to experience all manner of oil and grease spills here. And if your floor is made from porous, unsealed cement—and it probably is—the surface will absorb odors like a brand-new sponge.

1. The simplest way to remove odors is to pick up a large pail of nonclumping kitty litter.

2. Blot any oil or grease from the surface with newspaper; the floor should be fairly dry.

3. Spread a healthy amount of kitty litter on the stain, and using a broom, sweep it over the area until it's covered.

4. Let it stand for 24 hours, and sweep or vacuum up the litter. Magic!

RID RUST WITH VINEGAR

If you want to clean up those rusted old tools you recently unearthed under your house or picked up at a garage sale, soak them in full-strength white vinegar for several days. The same treatment is equally effective at removing the rust from corroded nuts and bolts. And you can pour vinegar on rusted hinges and screws to loosen them up for removal.

REVIVE YOUR PAINTBRUSHES

To remove dried-on paint from a synthetic-bristle paintbrush tossed in the garage, soak it in full-strength white vinegar until the paint dissolves and the bristles are soft and pliable, and wash in hot, soapy water. Does a paintbrush seem beyond hope? Before tossing it, try boiling it in 1 to 2 cups (250 to 500 ml) vinegar for 10 minutes, followed by a thorough washing in soapy water.

A SOLUTION FOR GREASY HANDS

To remove car grease or paint from your hands, pour 1 teaspoon (5 ml) olive oil and 1 teaspoon (5 ml) salt or sugar into your palms. Vigorously rub the mixture into your hands and between your fingers for several minutes, and wash it off with soap and water. Your hands will be clean, and softer as well.

CLEAN OIL AND GREASE FROM FABRIC

For an effective automotive oil and grease stain remover, pour 4 cups (1 L) cola over the fabric stain. For severe stains, soak garment in cola overnight. Rinse and launder the next morning.

KEEP MICE OUT OF THE RV

The access slots where you hook up your RV to a cable or hose are "step this way" entries for mice and other small critters. To take up the welcome mat in one fell swoop, wrap the cable or hose in steel wool before connecting it, making sure that the scratchy material seals the surrounding gap. With their entry barred, varmints will leave you in peace.

MAKE YOUR CAR GLEAM

USE VINEGAR INSTEAD OF WAX

You have time to wash your car at home yourself—but not the whole afternoon to spend waxing it. Skip the wax step and use vinegar instead. A teaspoon (5 ml) of undiluted white vinegar in the bucket of soapy wash water will help remove road grit and tar from the paint. When you fill the bucket with clean water for rinsing, add another teaspoon (5 ml) of vinegar; pour this blend all over the car. For an added touch, wipe down windows with vinegar to repel rain and frost.

GET WAX OFF RUBBER WITH PEANUT BUTTER

If you're waxing your car and you accidentally get white wax on black rubber trim or moldings, wipe the area with peanut butter. The rubber will revert to its original blackness.

REMOVE TAR FROM YOUR CAR

It may look pretty bad, but it's not that hard to get road tar off a car without damaging the paint. Make a soft paste

DIY BASIC CAR WASH

Taking your car to a commercial car wash can be a costly habit to maintain—and the results aren't as satisfying as when you do it yourself. This soap is tough on grime but gentle on your car's finish and your wallet.

- ½ **cup (125 ml) mild dishwashing liquid**
- ½ **cup (125 ml) baking soda**
  About 1 gal. (4 L) warm water

Mix ingredients in a clean gallon (4 L) container with lid. Shake until all baking soda is dissolved.

To use, mix 1 cup (250 ml) of the solution into a bucket of warm water.

of 3 parts baking soda to 1 part water and apply to the tar spots with a damp cloth. Let it dry for 5 minutes, then rinse clean.

BANISH BACK-ROAD DIRT

In many rural areas, so-called oil roads (some unpaved, others semi-paved) are sprayed with oil to control blowing sand and dust. If you find yourself driving along one of these back roads, your windshield may end up coated with oily grime. To cut through the muck, sprinkle cream of tartar over the windshield, then wipe the glass down with soapy water, rinse well and dry.

TAKE SAP OFF AUTO PAINT

Did you park your new car under a pine tree in spring? Or was a fresh Christmas tree strapped to the roof of your car in winter? You may think you'll never get all that sap off. It's utterly impervious to soap and water, and you certainly don't want to scrub with anything abrasive. Mayonnaise is your car's new best friend. Rub a generous dab directly on each sap

Let That Chrome Shine

If you want to give the chrome on your car a shine to end all shines, simply dampen a clean soft cloth with full-strength white vinegar and gently polish the surface to bring out the natural shine of the chrome.

Another method to shine up chrome is to take a damp pad of ultrafine steel wool (grade 0000) and squeeze it into a bowl containing a little baking soda, mixing with the steel wool until a paste forms. Scrub the chrome trim, rims and bumpers on your car with the steel wool, making small circles. Rinse the metal and wipe it dry with a clean soft cloth.

If the chrome is developing small rust spots, you can remove them by rubbing the area with a crumpled piece of aluminum foil dipped in cola. It really works!

deposit and let it sit for 10 minutes. Use a soft, absorbent rag to remove the mayo and sap, then wash the car as usual. This same treatment will also remove road tar that can accumulate on the fenders. Now, don't park under any trees again!

FREEZE THE STICKY STUFF
Another way of getting rid of sap is to press an ice cube over the sap for a minute or so. When the sap hardens, simply peel it off your car, bicycle or other surface.

CLEAN WIPER BLADES

When your windshield actually gets blurrier after you turn on your wipers during a rainstorm, it usually means that the wiper blades are dirty. To make them as good as new, dampen a cloth or rag with some full-strength white vinegar and run it down the full length of each blade once or twice.

KEEP WIPERS ICE FREE

Getting into a cold car isn't the worst part of keeping your car outside in cold weather—frozen windshield wiper blades may take that award. Prevent ice by washing blades with a soft clean cloth doused in rubbing alcohol.

CLUB SODA VS. RUST

To loosen rusty nuts and bolts, pour some club soda over them. The carbonation helps to bubble the rust away.

GET RID OF CAR BATTERY CORROSION

If your car battery has corrosion on the terminals, dip a rag in cola and wrap it around the terminals. Let it sit for several minutes and then scrub off the rust deposits and any cola residue with a damp sponge.

SHED OLD BUMPER STICKERS

To remove those cutesy stickers your kids used to decorate your car bumper, use a blow-dryer on its hottest setting to soften the adhesive. Move the dryer slowly back and forth for several minutes. Next, use your fingernail or a credit card to lift up a corner and slowly peel the sticker off.

UPHOLSTERY

CARE FOR CAR CARPET

A good vacuuming will get up the sand and other loose debris from your car's carpeting, but it won't do much for stains or ground-in dirt. For that, mix a solution of equal parts water and white vinegar and sponge it into the carpet. Give the mixture a couple of minutes to sink in, then blot it with a cloth or paper towel. This technique will also eliminate salt residues left on car carpets during the winter months in snow areas.

MAGIC CLEANER FOR GREASE

No matter how meticulous you are, you'll

eventually end up with greasy stains on the carpet inside your car. When the inevitable happens, mix equal parts of salt and baking soda and sprinkle the mixture over the grease spot. Use a stiff brush to work the powdery white stuff into the spot, and let it sit four or five hours. Vacuum it up, and no more stain!

BRUSH OFF SAND

Keep a clean, dry paintbrush in your car specifically for those return trips from the beach. Use it to remove sand from beach chairs, towels, toys, the kids and yourself before you open the car door or trunk. You'll wind up with a lot less to vacuum the next time you clean your vehicle.

RECIPE: NATURAL UPHOLSTERY SHAMPOO

Use to freshen up fabric interiors that get a lot of use. It's cheaper than commercial upholstery cleaners, and it does the job.

- 6 Tbsp. (90 ml) pure soap flakes (or a bar of pure soap)
- 2 Tbsp. (30 ml) borax
- 2 cups (500 ml) boiling water

If you cannot find pure soap flakes, lightly grate a bar of pure soap on a coarse kitchen grater.

In a large bowl, mix the soap flakes and borax together. Slowly add the boiling water, stirring well to thoroughly dissolve the dry ingredients.

Let the mixture cool, then whip into a foamy consistency with an eggbeater.

Brush dry suds onto the upholstery, concentrating on soiled areas. Quickly wipe off with a damp sponge.

Upholstery Upkeep

Yes, you can make your own cleaners for car seats (and perhaps put the money you save toward a fun road trip). Here are two additional recipes, one for vinyl upholstery and the other for leather.

VINYL SHINER

- ¼ cup (60 ml) liquid soap
- ½ cup (125 ml) baking soda
- 2 cups (500 ml) warm water

Mix together liquid soap, baking soda and warm water.

Dip a clean cloth in the mixture and wipe the seats and trim, then rinse with clear water.

If you encounter any tough spots, rub them with a paste made from baking soda and water; let the paste soak in for an hour or more, then wash the entire area with the cleaner and rinse it.

LEATHER LUXURIATOR

- ½ cup (125 ml) rubbing alcohol
- ½ cup (125 ml) white vinegar
- 1 ½ cups (375 ml) water

Mix together rubbing alcohol, vinegar and water.

Soak a soft cloth in the solution and clean the upholstery with a circular rubbing motion before buffing it dry.

CAR ODORS

FRESHEN CAR AIR

The air in your car is getting a bit stale. The trick is to plan ahead and bring a bag filled with cotton balls soaked in pure vanilla extract, tea tree oil or eucalyptus oil. Take out a couple, put them in the car's cup holder, and enjoy a natural scent that's subtler than that of overperfumed or synthetic commercial air fresheners.

TRY THIS ODOR-EATING PAIRING

Deodorize the interior of your car by sprinkling baking soda over everything but the electronic equipment. Take a soft-bristled brush and work it in well. Close the car up for an hour or so, and then thoroughly vacuum the interior. To keep the car smelling fresh and clean, place a small open container of freshly ground coffee where it won't be disturbed. The grounds will absorb any strong odors.

ERADICATE A CARSICK SMELL

Young riders sometimes become carsick. Once you've cleaned up every trace, you may still smell the odor, making everyone else feel carsick, too! Leave a half-full uncovered bowl of undiluted white vinegar on the floor of the car overnight. In the morning, the odor should be gone.

DEODORIZE A CAR TRUNK

Stop holding your breath every time you open your car trunk. Instead, soak a slice of white bread in white vinegar and leave it in the malodorous space overnight. The smell should be gone by morning.

FIGHT SKUNK SCENT

Dissolve 1 cup (250 ml) dried mustard in 3 gallons (11.5 L) water and splash it over a skunky car's tires and undercarriage, using a spray wand to clean the latter.

SEE OUT YOUR WINDOWS

ICE PREVENTION

Use salt water to simplify scraping your car windows. Before a snowstorm, wipe your windows with a sponge dipped in salt water, then let them dry. The salt will discourage ice formation on the windows during the storm. The next time you go out to your car, the windows shouldn't be coated with ice.

STAY FROST-FREE

If you park your car outdoors during the cold winter months, a smart and simple way to stop frost from forming on windows is by wiping (or, better yet, spraying) the outsides of the windows with a solution of 3 parts white vinegar to 1 part water. Each coating may last up to several weeks.

DIY WINDSHIELD CLEANER

You shouldn't have to buy commercial windshield cleaner. Keep a spray bottle of this solution in your trunk (along with some old newspaper to wipe off the grime). Be sure to wipe off any solution that gets on rubber or plastic gaskets or wipers with a damp cloth because prolonged contact with alcohol may damage them.

3   cups (750 ml) glycerin
1   cup (250 ml) rubbing alcohol
2   cups (500 ml) water
1   clean 48-oz. (1.5 L) repurposed spray bottle

Combine the liquid ingredients in the spray bottle and shake well before using.

TRY AN ONION BAG HACK

Use old onion bags to clean bugs off your windshield. The mesh gives you enough of an edge to scrape the gunk off, but it won't damage the glass. Apply a mixture of dishwashing liquid and warm water to the windshield to soften everything up, scrub with the bags, and then wipe dry.

SAY BYE TO BUGS WITH PEANUT BUTTER

Another option to clean dead bugs off your windshield or bumper is to smear the area with peanut butter and let it sit to soften the bug splatters. Wash off the mess with a cloth soaked in soapy water.

REPEL RAIN FROM A WINDSHIELD

You know you need new wiper blades, but now there's rain in the forecast and you haven't replaced them yet. Dissolve a couple of tablespoons (about 30 ml) baking soda in 2 cups (500 ml) water, dip in a clean cloth and rub it over the windshield. Rain will slip off more easily until you buy new blades.

BIRD POO VOODOO

Have birds used your windshield as a target? Pour vinegar onto a rag and wipe those messes away with ease. Have winged friends left "gifts" on your patios and decks? Pour a little vinegar straight onto the spots and watch them dissolve like magic too.

DROPPINGS ON THE GO

Another option for bird messes on your car is to keep a spray bottle filled with club soda in the trunk and use it to help remove bird droppings or greasy stains from your windshield when on the road.

GARDEN AND PESTS

IN THE GARDEN

USE SALT TO STOP WEEDS

Those weeds that pop up in the cracks of your paths can be tough to eradicate. But salt can do the job. Bring a solution of about 1 cup (250 ml) salt and 2 cups (500 ml) water to a boil. Pour directly on the weeds to kill them. Another equally effective method is to spread salt directly on the weeds or unwanted grass that come up between patio bricks or blocks. Sprinkle with water or just wait until rain does the job for you.

MIX A NATURAL REMEDY

Be kind to the environment—not so much to weeds—by using a natural weed killer rather than harmful herbicides. Mix 1 teaspoon (5 ml) of dishwashing liquid with 1 cup (250 ml) of salt and 1 gallon (4 L) of white vinegar. Pour the solution on weeds sprouting in the cracks and crevices of sidewalks, front walks and patio pavers.

KEEP WEEDS OUT WITH BAKING SODA

Another safe way to keep weeds and grasses from growing in cracks is to sprinkle a few handfuls of baking soda on the concrete and simply sweep it into the cracks. The added sodium will make it much less hospitable to dandelions and their friends.

EXTERMINATE DANDELIONS AND UNWANTED GRASS

Make dandelions disappear for good by spraying each with full-strength white or apple cider vinegar. Early in the season, give each plant a single spray of vinegar in its midsection, or in the middle of the flower before the plants go to seed. Aim another shot near the stem at ground level so the vinegar can soak down to the roots. Keep an eye on the weather, though; if it rains the next day, you'll need to give the weeds another spraying.

Ground Cover to the Rescue

Don't run the risk of damaging the soil for the plants you have nurtured by using chemical weed killers. You'll find there is no need to use them when you think in terms of the right ground cover.

Plants that rob weeds of light and nutrients through their own growth are an environmentally friendly way to control weeds. Ground cover plants are especially useful.

Use dense-growing ground cover plants such as wild strawberries, periwinkles and violets for shady areas.

Prevent weeds from growing in sunny beds by planting sedums, euphorbias and ground cover roses.

Mulch between plants to prevent unwanted weeds from coming to the surface. For mulch, use freshly cut grass, wood chips, lucerne or sugar cane; in rock gardens you can also use gravel.

Sow plants that nourish the soil. This also suppresses weeds and will later contribute to healthy growth in the flower bed.

To prevent the growth of weeds in larger or inaccessible areas of the garden, cover thick layers of newspaper with mulch and cut crosses into the newspaper through which desirable plants can emerge (or into which they can be planted).

REMOVE MOSS FROM FLAGSTONES
Pour white vinegar straight over mossy flags and scrub off the moss with a wire brush. The brush will remove the existing moss, and the vinegar will help kill off the spores. If the flags are set in a very damp, shady area, the moss will inevitably creep back, but if it has merely crept into an area where you don't want it, a wire brush and vinegar should do the trick.

FERTILIZER, FREE FOR THE ASKING

Healthy plants are naturally resistant to insects and diseases, and natural fertilizers are the best way to ensure healthy plants and a balanced garden ecosystem. No matter where you live, good sources of fertilizer may be available, free for the hauling, at farms and from neighbors who have pet rabbits or chickens. All you have to do is ask for animal manure to enrich your compost.

BANANA PEELS FOR THE GARDEN

Dispose of banana peels properly to keep fruit flies away. Banana peels are one of the most common bearers of fruit-fly larvae. If you're a banana eater and you have a big problem with fruit flies, keep the peels out of the compost and bury them, cut up, directly in the soil around the plants you want to fertilize. They're a good source of potassium, and are beneficial to flowering plants such as roses—but don't bury more than three skins per rosebush per week.

GROW ROSE COMPANIONS

Provide roses with at least one botanical companion that will help keep many pests away. Lavender, rosemary and thyme repel aphids; French marigolds kill nematodes; chives help prevent powdery mildew; and the sulfur in garlic and onions wards off fungus growth.

ROSE BLACK SPOT FUNGICIDE

It's long been known that roses grown next to tomatoes are less likely to fall victim to black spot. Make a fungicide by snipping tomato leaves from a plant and whirring them in a blender with a little water; use enough leaves to make 2 cups (500 ml) of slurry. Combine with 1½ quarts (1.5 L) water and 2 tablespoons (30 ml) cornstarch and mix well. Store the solution in the fridge, marking it with a warning label. Spray your rosebushes once a week with the fungicide.

Soil Conditioners

Improve your garden soil with these true-to-nature items.

SEAWEED SOIL CONDITIONER

Seaweed is actually higher in nitrogen and potassium than most animal manures and is also a rich source of trace elements. Check if beachside municipalities are happy to have you haul it away.

Seaweed

To cleanse seaweed of salt, pile it where runoff will be directed to a storm drain, such as on your driveway. Allow several rains to rinse away the sea salt, then add the seaweed to your compost pile or dig it into garden beds in the autumn.

To make seaweed tea, steep an old pillowcase filled with seaweed in a bucket of water for 1 week. Remove and discard the pillowcase, dilute the liquid to the color of weak tea, and water your plants with it.

COFFEE GROUNDS FERTILIZER

Acidic coffee grounds make an excellent soil conditioner or mulch for acid-loving plants such as conifers, azaleas and rhododendrons. You can often have as much of the used grounds as you need, free for the taking, from your local cafe.

Coffee grounds

Apply a 3-inch-thick (8 cm) mulch of coffee grounds around the base of acid-loving plants, leaving a 6-inch (15 cm) ring of bare soil around the trunk of the plant to discourage fungal collar-rot diseases and trunk-eating insects.

For a complete fertilizer with a 2-4-2 analysis, mix 4 parts coffee grounds with 1 part composted wood ashes, and work into soil in autumn.

Stop Fungus Problems

Try one of these simple tricks to put an end to pesky fungi on your plants.

ANTIFUNGAL COMPOST TEA

Compost is not just a great soil conditioner and fertilizer. It also contains beneficial organisms that resist soil-borne fungal diseases. To discourage the formation of fungus on plants, such as brown patch, sooty mildew and powdery mildew, make a "tea" treatment using common garden compost.

1   gal. (4 L) bag compost
1   empty burlap bag or
     old pillowcase
     String
2½ gal. (10 L) water

Place compost in the bag, tie the bag shut with string and drop it into a bucket of water.

Set the bucket in a sunny spot, and steep the bag in the water for 2 or 3 days—until the water turns dark brown.

Remove the bag of compost (use contents as mulch). Dilute the remaining solution with water to the color of weak tea. Spray it on roses, zinnias, phlox and other plants that are susceptible to fungal infections. Repeat twice monthly during the growing season to prevent outbreaks.

BAKING SODA FUNGAL FIX

Apply to fungus-prone plants, such as roses, before they show signs of mildew, to prevent diseases such as powdery and sooty mildew and black spot. To further discourage fungal diseases, keep plant leaves as dry as possible by watering the soil without splashing the leaves, and mulch plants with compost.

1   tsp. (5 ml) baking soda
1   tsp. (5 ml) dishwashing
     liquid (do not use laundry
     or dishwasher detergent)
4   cups (1 L) warm water

Pour the ingredients into a large repurposed spray bottle and shake to mix. Spray both sides of leaves and stems.

TREAT RUST AND OTHER PLANT DISEASES

You can use vinegar to treat a host of plant diseases, including rust, black spot and powdery mildew. Mix 2 tablespoons (30 ml) apple cider vinegar in 2 quarts (2 L) of water and pour some into a repurposed spray bottle. Spray the solution on your affected plants in the morning or early evening (when temperatures are relatively cool and the plant has no direct light) until the condition is cured.

 Insider Tip

If you plant ferns, lamb's lettuce or tansy, ants will avoid your garden rather than enter it.

KILL POISON IVY

It's hard to fully destroy this dangerous vine once it takes hold, but salt will do the trick. Dissolve 3 pounds (1.4 kg) of sidewalk salt in 1 gallon (4 L) of water and add a squirt of dish liquid. Saturate the plant and its roots, being cautious about surrounding soil and plants. The poison ivy will soon be gone.

CLEAN CLAY POTS EASILY

Scrub off the unattractive white lime deposits on the outside of clay pots with vinegar and water. To prevent the deposits from returning, apply only water that has aerated for 24 hours.

THE NO-WATER CLEANSE

When you need to clean out a flowerpot for reuse, instead of making a muddy mess by washing the pot in water, just sprinkle in a little salt and scrub off the dry dirt with a stiff brush. This method is especially handy if your potting bench is not near a water source.

DON'T FRET OVER LOST GLOVES

If your garden gloves have gone missing and you need a quick fix, just scrape your fingernails over a bar of soap before digging in the garden. The dirt will come out from under your nails more easily when you scrub your hands.

RECIPE: RUST REMOVER

Use vinegar as a rust remover for old hinges, screws and metal garden furniture exposed to the elements.

White vinegar
Paper towels
Steel wool

Fill a wide-mouthed jar half full of vinegar, drop in small rusty parts, screw the lid on and soak for a few days until rust loosens. Remove the objects, rinse and carefully dry.

Soak a paper towel in vinegar and lay it over furniture surfaces to loosen rust. If the rust is stubborn, cover the saturated towel with plastic wrap to keep the towel damp. Set the piece out of direct sunlight for a few days. Remove the wrapping, steel-wool the spot smooth, rinse and dry. Paint if desired.

DIRTY HANDS NO MORE!

Been gardening and can't get that dirt scrubbed off your fingertips? Mix oatmeal—either quick-cooking or old-fashioned, but not the flavored instant kind—with enough milk to make a thin paste, and scrub your hands well with it. The dirt will come out, and your hands will feel softened and smooth.

MAKE BIRD DROPPINGS VANISH

Have birds been using your patio or driveway for target practice again? Get rid of droppings by spraying them with full-strength apple cider vinegar. Or pour the vinegar on a rag and wipe droppings off.

HUMMINGBIRD FEEDER CARE

Don't expect to see hummingbirds flocking around a dirty, sticky or crusted-over sugar-water feeder. Regularly clean feeders by thoroughly washing them in equal parts apple cider vinegar and hot water. Rinse well with cold water after washing and air-dry them outdoors in full sunlight before refilling them.

CHECK ON THAT COMPOST PILE

If the compost pile has a strong smell, the problem is most likely either too much moisture or too much nitrogen-rich green material. Be sure to balance the mixture properly between green material and brown, carbon-based material such as dead leaves, hay or straw. Turn the pile regularly to further blend the contents and keep annoying fruit flies and fungus

Quick Guide: Clean Outdoor Furniture and Decks

Before you reach for the bleach, try one of these milder cleaning solutions:

Keep full-strength white vinegar in a repurposed spray bottle and use it wherever you see any mildew growth. The stain will wipe right off most surfaces and the vinegar will keep it from coming back for a while.

To deodorize and inhibit mildew growth on outdoor plastic-mesh furniture and patio umbrellas, mix 2 cups (500 ml) white vinegar and 2 tablespoons (30 ml) dishwashing liquid in a bucket of hot water. Use a soft brush for scrubbing seat pads and umbrella fabric. Rinse with cold water and dry in the sun.

Most commercial cleaners are too abrasive to be used on resin garden furniture. But you won't have to worry about scratching or dulling the surface if you clean your resin furniture with a wet sponge dipped in baking soda. Wipe using circular motions and rinse well.

---

gnats from swarming to it. Keep the compost covered to keep moisture out.

PAPER AND WOOD TO COMPOST

Compost paper, cardboard and sawdust from untreated wood. Shred paper first, and break cardboard down into a slurry by ripping it to pieces and adding water. Tissues and paper towels can also be composted without any special treatment. Avoid glossy paper and sawdust from pressure-treated wood. (Pressure-treated wood can leak arsenic into soil—not ideal for vegetable gardens.)

 Take Care Rats and mice love compost, and they attract snakes, which prey on them. A tumbling compost bin on a frame won't let them in.

LAWN CARE

PLANT THE RIGHT KIND OF GRASS

If you've got the wrong kind of grass, you may have trouble maintaining a lush lawn. Traditional bluegrass has a shallow root structure and can be hard to keep healthy. Grasses with deeper roots—such as tall fescue or red fescue—require less watering and are less susceptible to disease. If you already have bluegrass and don't want to dig it up and start over, try overseeding it in spring or fall with another (hardier) bluegrass variety.

TREAT YOUR LAWN WITH HOUSEHOLD LIQUIDS

Fill the reservoir of a 10- or 20-gallon (38 or 76 L) hose-end sprayer with water, 1 cup (250 ml) of dishwashing liquid and one of the following: a 12-ounce (350 ml) can of beer or non-diet cola, 1 cup (250 ml) of corn syrup or molasses, or ½ cup (125 ml) mouthwash. The dishwashing liquid helps spread the concoction more evenly across your lawn, and as an added bonus, helps it stick to individual blades of grass. Water your lawn approximately every 3 weeks, and watch your neighbors turn green with envy—to match your lawn.

YELLOW LAWN SPOTS COULD MEAN LOW AREAS

Not every yellow spot on your lawn was caused by a pest. Many of these spots just need a little bit of compost. A low spot in your lawn can also turn yellow, especially after a heavy rain. If that's the problem, putting a little soil over the indentation to raise it up to the level of the surrounding ground will fix it.

WATER YOUR DOG'S FAVORITE SPOTS MORE OFTEN

Yellow patches in your lawn could be caused by the nitrogen in your dog's urine. Even though fertilizers contain nitrogen, the concentration that is emitted in a dog's urine is too much for grass to take. The way to solve this problem is to dilute the urine after it hits the lawn. Water that spot within 8 hours of the deposit to stop yellow circles from forming.

Handy Hack

Pour salt on lawn weeds or sprinkle them with a solution of 1 part vinegar to 1 part water.

HONE IN ON HOUSEPLANTS

PHOTO-WORTHY HOUSEPLANTS

Even a healthy houseplant looks sad and dingy when the leaves are coated with a fine layer of dust. Make the whole house look as verdant as a florist's shop by rubbing each leaf with a cloth dipped in a little mayonnaise. Polish each leaf off with another cloth and you'll have a gleaming, deep green shine that will last for months.

DO A QUICK DUSTING

Put on old cloth gardening gloves and run your fingers over the tops and

bottoms of each leaf simultaneously. You'll have dusted the entire plant in no time!

Handy Hack

Wipe all of your larger-leafed houseplants with diluted beer (yes, beer!) to make them shine.

GIVE CACTI SPECIAL ATTENTION

Gentle is the way to go when dusting potted cacti, so brush them lightly with an old soft toothbrush or shaving brush. In summer, spray the plants lightly with water after brushing.

GOT SILK FLOWERS OR ARTIFICIAL HOUSEPLANTS?

They may require less care than their living counterparts, but silk flowers and artificial houseplants are apt to collect dust and dirt. Use a blow-dryer on its highest, coolest setting for a quick, efficient way to clean them off. Since this will blow the dust onto the furniture surfaces and floor around the plant, do this either outside or just before you vacuum those areas.

OUTDOOR PESTS

SHIELD YOUR VEGETABLE GARDEN

For centuries, gardeners have used companion planting to repel insect pests. Aromatic plants such as basil, tansy, marigolds and sage are all said to repel pests, so try planting some near your vegetables. Mint, thyme, dill and sage are favored near cabbage-family plants (cabbage, broccoli, cauliflower and Brussels sprouts) for their supposed ability to fend off cabbage moths. And a bonus: You can eat the savory herbs!

MAKE A NONPOISONOUS TRAP

If insects are feasting on the fruits and vegetables in your garden, give them the boot with this simple, nonpoisonous trap. Fill a 2-liter (2 qt.) soda bottle with 1 cup (250 ml) apple cider vinegar and 1 cup (250 ml) sugar. Slice a banana peel into small pieces, put them in the bottle, add 1 cup (250 ml) cold water and shake it. Tie a piece of string around the neck of the bottle and hang it from a low tree branch, or place it on the ground, to trap the freeloaders. Replace used traps with new ones as needed.

STOP APHIDS IN THEIR TRACKS

Plant fennel or cilantro between plants to protect shrubs. For roses, you can plant

Secret Resource: Your Spice Rack

We love our herbs and spices, but most garden pests find them unpalatable or even lethal. Sprinkle any of the following examples around your plants and watch leaf-hungry pests go in search of another spot to dine.

Powdered cinnamon
Powdered cloves
Cayenne pepper
Black pepper
Chili powder

Hot curry powder
Garlic powder
Dried lemon thyme
Dried bay leaves, crumbled

Spray Your Plants

Got an insect problem? Use one of these plant-friendly mixes to keep them at bay.

DIY NATURAL PESTICIDE

Make an effective insect repellent for your garden with these simple ingredients you likely have at home.

- 4   onions
- 2   garlic cloves
- 2   Tbsp. (30 ml) cayenne pepper
- 1   qt. (1 L) water
- 2   Tbsp. (30 ml) soap flakes
- 2   gal. (7.5 L) water

In a blender, puree onions, garlic, cayenne pepper and 1 quart (1 L) water. Set this aside.

Now dilute soap flakes in 2 gallons (7.5 L) water. Pour in the contents of the blender, and shake well, and you have a potent, earth-friendly solution to spray on your plants.

RECIPE: ALCOHOL INSECT TREATMENT

Rubbing alcohol is a tried-and-true homemade treatment for soft-bodied garden pest insects such as aphids and mealybugs. You can dab it onto insects with a cotton swab, but this is time-consuming. Try this speedy spritz instead.

- 1   cup (250 ml) rubbing alcohol
- 1   cup (250 ml) water

Combine the alcohol and water in a repurposed spray bottle and shake to combine.

Before treating, spray one leaf of the infested plant as a test to make sure it has no reactions, such as browning. If not, spray the entire plant, including the undersides of leaves and flower buds. Avoid spraying open flowers, which may turn brown if treated with alcohol.

Repeat every other day for 3 days to kill hatchlings. Monitor plants and spray again as needed. Label the bottle and store it out of the reach of children and pets.

garlic, lavender or French marigolds. If plants are already infested, spray them in the morning with a strong jet of water. A spray made from tansy or nettle tea will also help. Encourage ladybugs in the garden—their larvae devour aphids.

FIGHTING APHIDS WITH TANSY

Use this simple combination to rid your garden of these pests.

1   cup (250 ml) fresh or 2 Tbsp. (30 ml) dried tansy leaves
1   qt. (1 L) water

Boil the leaves in water and steep for 1 hour.

Dilute the tea with water in a 1:1 ratio and spray on affected plants. Or pour or spray a tansy slurry made of 1¼ cups (300 ml) of fresh leaves and 10 quarts (9.5 L) of water twice a week. Tansy is poisonous, so take special care around children and animals.

BANANAS VS. APHIDS

If aphids are attacking your rosebushes or other plants, bury dried or cut-up banana peels a few inches deep around the base of the plants, and the aphids soon will leave. Don't use whole peels or bananas themselves, though; they tend to be viewed as tasty treats by possums, raccoons, rabbits and other animals, which will just dig them up.

USE SCENTED MULCH

Trimming herbs frequently, especially removing flower stalks, helps them maintain lots of tender, flavorful new growth. Sprinkle the sprigs and flowers that you don't use in the kitchen along garden paths as aromatic and insect-repelling mulch.

LEAVE IT TO THE TOADS

Toads are among the most insect-hungry garden visitors. Attract them by placing a broken flowerpot or two in a shady spot, then sink a pan filled with water and rocks into the soil so any visiting toads will stick around.

TRY A LITTLE BLACK PEPPER

You don't have to use harsh pesticides to control a small insect infestation outdoors. If ants are swarming on your garden path, add 1 tablespoon (15 ml)

BLOCKING INSECTS WITH RHUBARB

Rhubarb is an attractive perennial plant that not only makes good pies but also makes an insecticide that is toxic to sucking insects. This recipe is for ornamental plants only. Do not spray on herbs, fruits or vegetables because rhubarb leaves are toxic to humans and animals.

3   **stalks rhubarb with leaves**
3½   **qt. (3.5 L) water**

Chop the rhubarb leaves and stems. In a stockpot, combine the rhubarb and water. Bring to a boil, reduce the heat and simmer, uncovered, for 1 hour.

Cool to room temperature and strain liquid into a repurposed spray bottle. Spray mixture on infested plants at 3-day intervals for 10 days. Repeat as necessary.

ground black pepper (or another strong-smelling ground spice, such as ground cloves or dry mustard) to 1 cup (250 ml) sifted white flour and sprinkle the mixture on and around the pests. They'll vanish within the hour. Sweep the dry mix into the garden instead of trying to hose it off; water will just make it gooey.

GIVE ANTS THE BOOT

Get rid of household ants once and for all by pouring equal parts water and white vinegar into a repurposed spray bottle, and spraying it on anthills and around areas where you see the insects. Ants hate the smell of vinegar, so it won't take long for them to move on. Also keep the spray bottle handy for outdoor trips or to keep ants away from picnics or children's play areas. If you have lots of anthills around your property, try pouring full-strength vinegar over them to hasten the insects' departure.

EXPERIMENT WITH ORANGE PEEL

Get rid of the ants in your garden, on your patio and along the foundation of your home. In a blender, make a smooth puree of a few orange peels in 1 cup (250 ml) warm water. Slowly pour the solution over and into anthills to send the little pests packing. Repeat if they return.

BLAST AWAY FIRE ANTS

If fire ants plague your yard or patio and you're tired of getting stung by the tiny attackers, a flowerpot can help you quench the problem. Place a flowerpot upside down over the anthill. Pour boiling water through the drain holes and you'll be burning down their house.

DIY OIL SPRAY INSECTICIDE CONCENTRATE

Some plant pests and fungal infections are hard to eradicate because they have shells or waxy coatings that protect them from traditional treatments. You can, however, smother tough shelled scale, the eggs of many insects and even mildew infections by coating them with oil. Store all garden treatments, such as this, in a sealed and labeled bottle in a childproof cabinet.

3   tsp. (15 ml) dishwashing liquid (do not use laundry or dishwasher detergent)
1   cup (250 ml) vegetable oil

In a pint (500 ml) container, combine the ingredients to form a spray concentrate. Store it in a sealed, labeled container.

To apply, mix 1 or 2 teaspoons (5 or 10 ml) of concentrate with 1 cup (250 ml) water in a repurposed spray bottle and apply to stems and both sides of plant leaves. Reapply after it rains.

Stop Slugs and Snails

The gastropod gourmets we know as slugs and snails have a special taste for dahlias, delphiniums, hostas, lupines, marigolds, zinnias and almost any flower or veggie seedling. Luckily, it's possible to deprive them of their meals.

Bury shallow containers (a jar lid is the usual choice) so that the rim is level with the soil, then fill it with beer. Slugs and snails love the yeast in beer and overindulge until they drown.

Take a container of salt into the garden and douse the offenders. They won't survive for long.

Make an unbroken ring of wood ashes around your favorite flowers. Slugs and snails will turn away from caustic ashes. Make sure to reapply ashes after it rains. You can also sprinkle small amounts of ash over garden plants to manage infestations of soft-bodied insects. Wear eye protection and gloves.

After enjoying half a grapefruit for breakfast, put the leftover rind upside down in the garden. Slugs and snails will gather under it, at which point you can smash the rind with the back of a shovel and add it (and the dead crawlers) to your compost pile. Other citrus rinds work, too.

Spread coffee grounds around garden beds—the caffeine they contain deters and poisons slugs and snails. Reapply after a rain.

Use gravel on garden beds. The sharp edges cut slugs on their soft underbellies, killing them.

Grow dahlias, verbena, hydrangea or marigolds in tubs so that snails can't get to them. Or secure copper bands around pots. Slugs and snails will be deterred by the feel and taste of the metal.

Sanding disks are perfectly sized to fit under pots. No slug enjoys oozing across an abrasive surface. Make sure the circumference is wider than that of your pot.

REPEL CATERPILLARS WITH ONION JUICE

Spray cabbage and other vegetables targeted by caterpillars with onion juice, and watch the pests take a detour. To make a spray, peel 2 medium onions, grate them into a large bowl and add 1 gallon (4 L) water. Let the mixture sit overnight, then strain it into a repurposed spray bottle. To make the plants smelly enough to repel the pests, you may need to spray the leaves twice.

 Insider Tip If your garden is a haven for insects, caterpillars, snails and slugs, spread a mulch over it made from cedar shavings and chips to repel these pests.

PREVENT KILLER WORMS

If your garden is about 250 square feet (23 sq. m), all you need is a 5-pound (2.3 kg) bag of sugar to keep nematode worms off all your plants. These microscopic parasites attack roots, destroying the plants and all your hard work. If your area is prone to nematodes, spread the sugar over the soil in the spring when you're preparing the ground, and the nematodes will never get started. Microorganisms feeding on the sugar will increase the organic matter in the soil, eliminating those nasty nematodes.

HUNT HORNWORMS WITH A HOSE

While hornworms are the largest of the vegetable garden caterpillars, they're also among the hardest to spot; their pale green color camouflages them as they chomp on the leaves of tomato, potato and pepper plants. To find them, turn your hose nozzle to the fine spray setting and direct at a plant. Any hidden hornworms will thrash about and reveal their whereabouts, at which point you can pick them off and drop them into a bucket of water. The hotter the day, the more of a shock the cold spray will be.

CHASE CABBAGE WORMS AWAY

Every gardener knows the frustration of cabbage worms gnawing away just as the big heads of cabbage are ready to be harvested. Stop worms in their tracks with a mix of 1 part salt and 2 parts flour, dusted around the cabbages every few days as harvest approaches.

PROHIBITIVE MEASURE FOR MOSQUITOES

Eliminate standing water outside the house to get rid of mosquitoes. A mosquito's hunting ground is within about 100 to 200 feet (30 to 60 m) of where she begins her life cycle. (Only egg-bearing females bite people.) Empty out kiddie pools, buckets and anything else that collects water. If you have a koi

Natural Mosquito Repellents

For those who prefer to avoid commercial mosquito repellents with DEET or other chemicals, a number of natural alternatives are readily available.

Pennyroyal essential oil, peppermint, vanilla, bay, clove, sassafras, lavender oil and cedar all have their adherents.

Hang up a cloth sprayed with a few drops of clove or laurel oil. Alternatively, pour the oil into small bowls or an oil lamp.

Try burning rosemary and sage at your next barbecue—some people swear it keeps mosquitoes at bay.

You may love the mild apple-like flavor of chamomile tea but mosquitoes absolutely hate it. Brew a very strong batch of chamomile tea and keep it in a repurposed spray bottle in the fridge. Before you relax in the backyard, spray exposed skin liberally. It's fragrant, potent and totally safe for children.

Fresh parsley or apple cider vinegar, rubbed on the skin, are also found to be effective mosquito deterrents.

Some people find that increasing their intake of onions or garlic in the summer—or rubbing a slice of onion over their exposed skin—is a good way to keep away mosquitoes and other biting insects. If you're not crazy about the idea of rubbing onions all over yourself, you may be happy to know that you can often get similar results by rubbing fresh orange or lemon peels over your exposed skin. Mosquitoes and gnats are totally repulsed by either scent.

Another popular homemade bug repellent is concocted from 1 tablespoon (15 ml) citronella oil, 2 cups (500 ml) white vinegar, 1 cup (250 ml) water and 1 cup (250 ml) of a base oil to bind it all together, such as grapeseed, almond or olive oil.

pond, keep the water pump in good order. A mosquito that breeds far away from you will bite far away from you, too.

A safe way to ward off mosquitoes is to pin used dryer fabric softener sheets onto clothing when outdoors. The scent repels the pests.

DIY REPELLENT SMOKE

This fragrant, herbal smoke will help to deter flies and mosquitoes at your next barbecue. However, it is a mild solution and extra protection should be used in areas with mosquito-transmitted diseases.

Fresh rosemary sprigs
Fresh basil sprigs
Fresh thyme sprigs

When you remove food from the barbecue, spread out a handful of pungent culinary herbs on the top rack where they will smoke, but not burn.

Allow the herbs to cook and release their fragrances.

WATCH OUT, WASPS!

Wasps make themselves scarce when they detect the smell of heated vinegar. Lemon slices studded with cloves will also keep them away.

EASY EARWIG TRAP

Although earwigs don't hurt people, these nocturnal feeders can nibble plants overnight. Try this nontoxic control method. This technique also works with slaters.

Several sheets of
used newspaper
String

Roll several thicknesses of newspaper into a tight cylinder and secure with string. Dampen the rolled paper and place on the soil near eaten plants.

Check the newspaper roll each morning to see if earwigs are hiding inside. If so, dispose of them in a securely tied trash bag and set out a new roll. Continue this routine until earwigs are under control.

Outsmarting Stinging Insects

You can avoid attracting stinging insects, such as bees, wasps and mosquitoes, by being careful about what you wear or how you smell while gardening or sitting on the patio. Here are some smart suggestions:

Stinging insects that strike during daylight hours are attracted to flower colors—red, pink, yellow, orange and purple—so wear clothes in cool shades of blue, green, black, gray or white for yard and garden work.

Many stinging insects are also attracted to floral and fruity scents, so forgo perfume, scented shampoo, scented hair conditioners and fragrant body lotions.

Stinging insects are often repelled by herbal scents. Wear a broad-brimmed hat in the garden and tuck sprigs of rosemary, chrysanthemum or marigold flowers into the brim to repel insects. Or, if you don't want to wear a hat, put the sprigs into the pocket of your T-shirt.

INDOOR PESTS

DISCOURAGE INSECTS IN CONTAINERS

Flour, sugar and paprika can all fall prey to ants and other insects. Keep them safe by slipping a bay leaf inside your storage containers. If you're concerned about the flour or sugar picking up a bay leaf flavor, tape the leaf to the inside of the canister lid. This trick works inside cupboards, too, where sachets of sage, bay, cinnamon sticks or whole cloves will smell pleasant while also discouraging ants.

RELY ON LEMONS

You don't need insecticides or ant traps to ant-proof your kitchen. Just give it the lemon treatment. First squirt some

DIY ANT TRAPS

Here's an easy, inexpensive way to round up the ants that begin to invade your house each summer.

3	cups (750 ml) water
1	cup (250 ml) sugar
4	tsp. (20 ml) borax
3	clean 8-oz. (250 ml) screw-top jars
	Cotton balls
	Old-style beer-can opener (that cuts V-shaped notches)

In a jug, mix the water, sugar and borax together. Loosely pack the jars half full of cotton balls and saturate the balls with the solution.

Pierce jar lids with the can opener, making two or three holes just large enough for ants.

Place the baited jars where ants are active, but make sure jars are out of the reach of pets and children. Attracted by the lethal sugar and boric acid mixture, ants will crawl into the traps.

lemon juice on door thresholds and windowsills. Then squeeze lemon juice into any holes or cracks where the ants are getting in. Finally, scatter small slices of lemon peel around the outdoor entrance. The ants will get the message that they aren't welcome.

Take Care

Chemical pesticides can be hazardous to your health, especially if they are gaseous and can therefore spread throughout the home. They are best avoided altogether in living rooms, bedrooms and kitchens. Try using baits or biological treatments (lures) instead to supplement proven physical measures such as sealing gaps in walls or floors, and vacuuming thoroughly to keep pests at bay.

GET RID OF ROACHES

Toxic chemicals work to get rid of roaches, but particularly if you have children or pets, you don't necessarily want to use commercial roach products in your house. Instead, scatter corners and behind cabinets with a small mix of half sugar and half baking soda for a nontoxic and highly effective "poison." The roaches come to eat the sugar, but also eat the baking soda and die. Replace often until the roaches disappear.

Ants: The Unwanted Visitors

Ants love accessible moist food, especially sweets and proteins. They usually invade homes from the outside; ant colonies send out food scouts first before dispatching large numbers of workers. Try one of these methods to be rid of them.

Ants follow a scent trail, marching in a line. Disrupt them by sprinkling dried mint leaves, crushed cloves or chili powder where they enter the house. Once they lose the scent trail they can no longer find their way in. Or, draw a line with a piece of chalk or baby powder through the ants' route. You can also put a thin line of cream of tartar in their path. The tiny gatecrashers won't be able to cross it. And it's all much safer than chemicals in your kitchen.

Wipe minor ant trails you find inside the home with diluted vinegar or lemon juice, or sprinkle with ammonium bicarbonate (also known as baker's yeast). Ants also dislike cinnamon.

Ants will gobble down baking soda sprinkled on the floor and feed it to their young. This causes their stomachs to rupture, reducing the pest population. They can't resist a solution of sugar, yeast and water, either, which has the same effect.

Another effective bait against ants is honey, water and syrup. Set the mix out in a shallow dish; ants get trapped in the sticky solution and die.

COCKROACHES AND WEEVILS

For a minor infestation, use a cloth moistened with wine or beer as bait. When the insects have gathered on the cloth, pour boiling water over it. Remove food supplies immediately if they become infested with weevils and wash out kitchen cupboards with vinegar and water.

TRY NUTMEG OR GUM

One or two whole nutmegs buried in a sack of flour or box of rice will help keep weevils and other tiny invaders out. Some people claim to have successfully repelled bugs by placing sticks of spearmint gum (unwrapped) at different points on the floor of the cabinet where susceptible foodstuffs are stored.

POP GOES THE WEEVIL

If your dried beans or peas are under attack by hungry weevils, add a bit of dried hot pepper to the storage container. They'll hotfoot it out of the box or bag in a flash.

PURGE BUGS FROM YOUR PANTRY

Do you have moths or other insects in your cupboard or pantry? Fill a small bowl with 1½ cups (375 ml) apple cider vinegar and add a couple of drops of

RECIPE: COCKROACH BAIT

Cockroaches are attracted to damp areas, such as under the kitchen sink, but this inexpensive solution will kill them if they eat it. Remember to store pest treatments, such as this, in sealed and labeled bottles in a childproof cabinet.

1	metal coffee can with plastic lid
1	old-style beer-can opener (that cuts V-shaped notches)
2	Tbsp. (30 ml) borax
3	tsp. (15 ml) flour
3	tsp. (15 ml) sugar

Punch holes around the base of the empty coffee can using the beer-can opener. Label the can "Cockroach Killer."

In a small bowl, mix the ingredients together. Put the mixture in the coffee can, snap on the lid and place it under the sink or wherever you've seen cockroaches. Lock the cupboard if you have children or pets.

Refill the can or create additional cans as necessary.

A Pest-Free Pantry

Common pantry pests such as moths, weevils and mites will happily make their home in foods such as flour, cornmeal, sugar, nuts, dried fruit and various cereal products. An infestation of these pests can occur no matter how clean you keep your kitchen. In many cases, it begins because the eggs of an unwelcome guest are already present in a product when we buy it. Take care when shopping to choose products that are in sound condition and that have undamaged packaging.

Check the food in your pantry for pest infestation about once every 4 weeks. At the first sign of a problem, throw the affected item out. If an item is obviously infested, you will need to clear out the entire shelf or, better yet, the entire pantry. Dispose of all the food first, then wash out the pantry with a solution of vinegar and hot water.

To prevent a plague of pests, keep food in well-sealed containers in dry, cool conditions. Clean and air out your pantry regularly.

Pests contaminate food with their droppings, strands of silk and shed skin. This can cause skin irritation, allergies and gastrointestinal illness. Pests can also carry fungi, bacteria, viruses and parasites. For all these reasons, affected food should not be consumed under any circumstances.

dishwashing liquid. Leave it in there for a week; it attracts the bugs, which will fall into the bowl and drown. Then empty the shelves and give the interior a thorough washing with dishwashing liquid or 2 cups (500 ml) baking soda in 1 quart (1 L) of water. Discard all wheat products (breads, pasta, flour, etc.), and clean canned goods before putting them back.

FREEZE THE BUGGERS
Some bug eggs are in the containers before you bring your groceries home and have yet to hatch. Kill off any eggs

chemicals. In a small saucepan, simmer 2 cups (500 ml) milk, ¼ pound (115 g) raw sugar and ¼ cup (60 ml) ground pepper for about 10 minutes, stirring occasionally. Pour into shallow dishes or bowls and set them around the kitchen, patio or anywhere the flies are a problem. The insects will flock to the bowls and drown!

by keeping your products in the freezer for the first day or two if possible.

FLY DETERRENTS

During summer months, keep food covered and use a blue tablecloth; flies avoid this color. The smell of basil, peppermint, lavender or tomato plants also wards off flies—they don't like the fragrances of these plants.

Insider Tip To keep pests such as moths and weevils out of your pantry, don't leave dry goods such as flour, cereals, pasta, rice and beans in their original packaging once they have been opened. Transfer the contents to a resealable container such as a screw-top glass jar. Products in glass jars, bottles or clear plastic containers need to be kept in a dark place.

SHOO FLIES!

To get rid of flies, set out bowls of vinegar; replace them daily. If preparing meat in the kitchen, coat meat with lemon balm or basil before grilling it and the flies will stay away.

MAKE A NONTOXIC FLY TRAP

Keep a kitchen free of flies with a homemade fly trap that uses no toxic

BREAK THE FRUIT FLY CYCLE

If you like to keep a bowl of ripe fruit in your kitchen, you will probably end up with a swarm of fruit flies to go with it. An orange studded with cloves may be the solution—the best place to put it is on the windowsill. Fruit flies will be drawn to the orange, as citrus fruit is

DIY FLYPAPER

Take a cue from housekeepers of old and trap flies with flypaper. Hang these sticky strips underneath top cabinets, in doorways and from window frames.

1	brown paper grocery bag
	String
	Tape
⅔	cup (160 ml) sugar
⅔	cup (160 ml) light corn syrup
⅔	cup (160 ml) water

Cut the bag into strips 1½ inches (4 cm) wide and 1 to 3 feet (30 to 91 cm) long. Cut 5-to-6-inch (13 to 15 cm) pieces of string and secure them to the top of strips with transparent tape.

Combine sugar, corn syrup and water in a heavy 2-quart (2 L) saucepan and bring the mixture to a boil over high heat.

Reduce the heat to medium and cook until the liquid thickens.

Use a pastry brush to coat the strips with the liquid, and then hang them.

one of their favorite places to lay eggs. It will cost you a piece of fruit a day as you will need to dispose of the orange and replace it with a new one, but you will get rid of the fruit flies as you break their breeding cycle.

FRUIT FLY CATCHER

Fill a small bowl with a little apple juice and vinegar, some water, and a dash of dishwashing liquid. This mixture will attract fruit flies and cause them to drown. Yellow or pale green bowls work best, as these resemble old fruit and sick plants.

QUICK SPRAY SAVES THE DAY

The next time you see fruit flies hovering

in the kitchen, get out a fine-misting spray bottle and fill it with rubbing alcohol. Spraying the little flies knocks them out and makes them fall to the floor, where you can sweep them up. The alcohol is less effective than insecticide, but it's a lot safer than spraying poison around your kitchen.

NO MORE ITCHY FLEA BITES

Pest fleas are usually either dog or cat fleas, with very thin adults. They may drop eggs in bedding or just about anywhere, and these and the hatchlings are easily vacuumed up. The larvae tend to feed on skin cells and fungi in bedding, carpets, floor gaps or soil.

Flea bites are not entirely harmless: fleas spread disease and parasites, including tapeworms. To rid your home of fleas, put a few drops of dishwashing soap and some water on a plate. Place the plate on the floor next to a lamp. Fleas love light and will jump onto the plate and drown. Wash any affected textiles in a hot wash (at least 140°F) and hang in the sun to dry or store them in your freezer for several weeks.

CEDAR WARDS OFF FLEAS

Keep fleas out of your house by adding cedar chips to the stuffing in your pet's

Fend Off Fruit Flies

No need to keep the fruit bowl empty on the kitchen countertop just because these unwanted guests tend to help themselves. Send them packing with one of the following:

Scatter a few mint or basil sprigs near fresh fruit when you set it out; fruit flies hate the smell and will stay clear.

Rub a little rubbing alcohol on a counter next to a bunch of

bananas or a ripening melon, tomato or avocado.

Pour apple cider into a jar or bowl, and fruit flies will be drawn to the sweet-smelling liquid, only to drown.

Clothes Moths?
Get Chemical-Free Protection

If you wish to avoid an unpleasant surprise when getting your warm wool sweaters out for winter, learning about moths and how to prevent or address a moth problem may prove helpful.

Clothes moths are troublesome pests whose larvae feed mainly on animal hair. That's why clothes made of wool, silk, fur and leather are particularly at risk. Moths eat the fibers of sweaters, shirts and coats, leaving numerous holes; they can also infest blended fabrics with a wool or silk base. The only fabrics they reject are those made purely of plant materials, such as cotton, hemp or linen.

Your best protection against moths is prevention. Moths love skin flakes and the scent of sweat, so try to hang only clean, washed clothes in your closet. Store valuable at-risk items inside cotton pillow cases or sealed in vacuum storage bags.

Plenty of proven home remedies prevent moth infestations. These annoying pests do not like the scent of lavender, cloves or cedar wood, for example, so placing a sachet of lavender or cloves (available from health-food shops, supermarkets or online) or cedar balls inside closets helps to keep them away.

Once cedar balls start losing their odor, rough up the surface with sandpaper to release more of their scent. You can also add some drops of cedar oil.

Another method to drive away moths is with small bags of dried citrus peel—moths dislike the citrus smell.

Check your clothes, air your closets and re-stack or rehang clothes regularly, as moths do

cont. on p. 186

cont. from p. 185

not like movement. Also make sure that vulnerable clothes are stored somewhere cool and dry, because moths like warm, moist environments.

If you have pets or small children, you should avoid using traditional moth balls, as naphthalene, one of the active ingredients, is highly toxic if inhaled or swallowed.

bedding. Keep them out of your dog's house, too, by hanging or nailing a cedar ring just inside the doghouse.

SAY BYE TO FLEAS

Try one of these other snappy natural options to rid your home of fleas. If they have taken up lodging in the sofa, sprinkle it with borax, leave overnight, then vacuum. In a cupboard, a dish of lemon slices will keep fleas away. If a rug is infested, sprinkle it with salt, let it work for a few hours, then vacuum.

DETER DUST MITES

Mites dislike both fresh air and light, so shake out bedding and blankets regularly. Vacuum rugs or beat them outside, and wash them frequently. If possible replace carpets with wooden floors or tiles.

VEGETABLES FOR WOOD LICE

To get rid of wood lice, leave hollowed-out potatoes or turnips as a lure. Crush them together with the wood lice that have crawled inside.

GOT CARPET BEETLES?

Vacuum regularly to stop hair and lint from providing food for carpet beetle larvae. Seal cracks in parquet flooring and spray neem oil (available from health product suppliers) along baseboards. This makes the larvae stop eating and prevents them from growing and reproducing. Be warned, it will take time.

Handy Hack

Try spraying rubbing alcohol where bedbugs thrive. It will kill some bugs on contact.

Solutions for Pesky Silverfish

These long-lived, slender, silvery insects with three tails live inside small crevices in moist areas and usually come out at night. An infestation may indicate a dampness problem, especially if you find them eating paper.

When you find silverfish, seal the cracks where they hide, and vacuum frequently to control them in the long term.

Silverfish simply can't abide diatomaceous earth. It rips apart their delicate silvery skin.

To get rid of silverfish, sprinkle a little borax on damp cloths and place in the bathroom or kitchen at night. In the morning, shake the cloths outside.

Another method is to grate a potato on a piece of newspaper to attract silverfish, then fold and throw newspaper away.

These pests frequent places with lots of moisture. Hang an aromatic sachet containing apple-pie spices (cinnamon, nutmeg and allspice), sage or bay leaves on a hook in your bathroom vanity and behind the washing machine, or keep a few in decorative baskets along baseboards.

ADVICE ON FUNGUS GNATS

The tiny, annoying flies that you sometimes see rising from potted plants are not fruit flies but fungus gnats, which cannot be trapped in fruit-fly traps. However, covering the soil with about ¼ inch (0.6 cm) of dry sand and watering the plants from the bottom instead of the top can be helpful in deterring them.

DETER LARGE ANIMALS

BUILD A HIGH FENCE

If you've already built a fence but you still see deer chomping on your tulips, you didn't make the fence high enough. Deer are excellent jumpers, so to keep them from bounding right in, be sure your fence is at least 8 feet (2.5 m) high.

USE CHICKEN WIRE

Are the deer tearing up your garden again? Stake chicken wire flat around the perimeter of your garden. Deer don't like to walk on it and it looks much better than the usual chicken-wire fencing.

CHOOSE PLANTS WISELY

You can preserve your yard by cultivating plants that deer don't like to eat. They aren't fond of highly aromatic herbs such as mint, lavender, thyme, rosemary and sage. Flowers that make unpopular deer snacks include begonias, ageratum, cornflower, marigolds, cleome and salvia. Deer also tend to steer away from plants with thorns. Ask your local nursery for other suggestions.

RECIPE: SOAP REPELLENT

This method works for some animals, such as deer. Deer dislike the smell of deodorant soap. Fresh bars of soap make an even stronger deterrent. One bar can protect a 9-square-foot (1 sq. m) area.

> Several bars or scraps of deodorant bath soap (not floral scented)
> Long nail, or drill with ⅛-inch (3 mm) bit, or sock
> String

Remove the soap from the wrapper. Make a hole in one end of the bar of soap with the nail or the drill and run a piece of string through the hole. If using soap scraps, drop them into the toe of an old sock and tie the open end closed with string.

Tie the soap (or soap-filled sock) to the branch of a shrub or tree with string or attach to a stake in the garden bed. Replace when rain diminishes the soap.

BAR SOAP SAYS "STAY AWAY"

Bar soap can serve the same purpose as chemical deer deterrents, without the nasty odors and toxins. Sprinkle soap shavings on the dirt or dissolve the soap in water and spray it on the plants; either of these will keep deer away. (Just make sure to redo it after it rains—as with any scent-based deterrents, the rain will wash the soap away.)

TRY A SPICY TRICK

Mix ¼ cup (60 ml) cayenne with warm water in a repurposed spray bottle and mist it over the plants that the deer seem to be zeroing in on. If you can find the hole in your yard where that pesky groundhog hides in between eating your flowers, pour a liberal amount of cayenne down the hole (groundhogs usually have a second hole, too, that you should find and anoint), and it will hastily make other habitation plans.

BRING THE HEAT

Everyone knows that hot peppers make your mouth burn. So if rodents are attacking your ornamental plants, the solution may be to make them too spicy for the pests. In fact, hot peppers are the basis for many commercial rodent repellents. Chop up the hottest pepper you can find (habanero is best) and

combine it with 1 tablespoon (15 ml) ground cayenne and 2 quarts (2 L) water. Boil the mix for 15 to 20 minutes, then let it cool. Strain it through cheesecloth, add 1 tablespoon (15 ml) dishwashing liquid and pour it into a repurposed spray bottle. Spray plants liberally every 5 days or so. The spray works best for rabbits, chipmunks and woodchucks, but can also deter deer.

DISCOURAGE OTHER ANIMALS

Some animals—including cats, deer, dogs, rabbits and raccoons—can't stand the scent of vinegar even after it has dried. You can keep these unauthorized visitors out of your garden by soaking several old

rags in white vinegar and placing them on stakes around your veggies. Resoak the rags every 7 to 10 days.

SHOO OFF SKUNKS AND RACCOONS WITH CAMPHOR

These two furry pests like to raid your lawn at night for grubs, worms and insects, especially after a rain. The evidence they leave behind? Little round holes. To make your lawn unattractive to the foragers, sprinkle the grass with camphor crystals—an all-natural alternative to toxic moth crystals.

RECIPE: GARLIC OPOSSUM REPELLENT

Opossums can be a great nuisance in the garden, but they hate the taste of garlic. Whip up this brew and they'll soon be feeding elsewhere. You can also use ground fresh chile peppers or fish sauce in the solution instead of garlic.

8   to 10 cloves garlic, crushed
4   cups (1 L) hot water

In a bowl, mix the crushed garlic into the hot water and allow to stand overnight.

Strain the mixture into a repurposed spray bottle and spray foliage. Repeat every few days (or after a rain) until the opossums get the message.

BLOCK THOSE GNAWERS

Mice, rats and even squirrels and bats are experts at finding every conceivable entry into the house. When you discover one of their entry points, stuff it full of steel wool. It is much more effective than foam or newspaper because even dedicated gnawers are unlikely to try to chew through such a sharp blockade.

MICE COMING INSIDE?

Peppermint oil is a scent that mice find unappetizing. Dab it on cotton balls and place them where mice enter. If you do decide to set traps, lure mice with peanut butter or chocolate.

TOSS THREAD, THWART BIRDS

You don't always have to buy netting at the garden center to protect ripening cherries and other tree fruit from birds. Just buy two to three spools of black thread. Stand beside the tree, grab the loose end of the thread, and toss the spool over the tree to a helper. (If you're

Keep Mice Out of the Garden

These rodents nibble on bulbs and corms, devour newly sown peas and beans, and attack stored fruit and vegetables if not well protected.

Cover newly planted seeds with twigs of barberry, rose or some other thorny shrub to keep mice away.

Toss seeds in wood ash before you plant them. Give bulbs and tubers the same treatment before storing them.

Plant mint near vulnerable plants—rodents do not like its aroma.

Get a cat. Its mere presence may be more than enough to deter the pests.

thinking this activity would be great for kids, you're right.) Continue tossing the spool back and forth until it is empty. The thread won't seal birds off from the tree, but once they hit it a time or two they'll look for their ripe fruit lunch elsewhere.

NO MORE CATS IN YOUR PLANTS

Kitty won't think of your garden as a toilet anymore if you spread a pungent mixture of orange peels and used coffee grounds around your plants. The mix acts as great fertilizer, too.

PET
CARE

KEEP YOUR PET AND YOUR SPACE HEALTHY

WASH THOSE EARS

If your pet constantly scratches its ears, it could indicate the presence of an irritation or ear mites. Ease the itch (and wipe out any mites) by using a cotton ball dipped in a solution of 1 teaspoon (5 ml) baking soda in 1 cup (250 ml) warm water to gently wash the insides of your pet's ears. Another option is a bit of vinegar. Swabbing your pet's ears with a cotton ball or soft cloth dabbed in a solution of 2 parts vinegar and 1 part water will keep them clean and help deter ear mites and bacteria. It also soothes minor itches from mosquito bites. WARNING: Do not apply undiluted vinegar to open lacerations. If you see a cut in your pet's ears, seek veterinary treatment.

SAY FAREWELL TO FLEAS

Fed up with those annoying fleas? Put a few drops of dishwashing liquid and some water on a plate and place the plate on the floor next to a lamp. Fleas love light, so they will jump onto the plate and drown in the liquid.

TRY A SCENTED FLEA COLLAR

Store-bought flea collars often carry an

COCKTAIL FLEA DIP

To check for fleas, comb your pet over a sheet of white paper. If black specks (flea dirt) drop onto the paper, treat the animal at once with this dip (double the recipe for large pets). There are many expensive flea dips around, but this one does not contain harsh chemicals. To get rid of flea eggs—and future infestations—wash the animal's bedding and vacuum your house thoroughly. This makes 1 treatment.

2	Tbsp. (30 ml) vodka or dry vermouth
1¾	pints (825 ml) water

In a large saucepan, stir alcohol into water and bring to a boil.

Remove from the heat, cover the pan and allow the solution to steep for 2 hours.

Rub the cooled solution into your pet's fur, rinse and comb out.

unpleasant odor, and you may hesitate to put a chemical-laden collar so close to your pet's skin. Fit your pet with a natural, pleasant-smelling flea collar instead. Rub a few drops of essential oil of tea tree, citronella, lavender, eucalyptus or scented geranium into an ordinary webbed or rope collar or a doggy bandanna, and refresh the oil weekly.

KILL FLEA EGGS WITH SALT

This flea killer takes a little time to work its magic. Sprinkle salt onto your carpets to kill flea eggs; let it sit for a day, then vacuum. Repeat the process a few days later to make sure you haven't missed any flea eggs. Each time you vacuum the salt, tie up and discard the vacuum bag.

Flea-Free with Common Items

Consider aromatic leaves, wood shavings and soap your first defense in your arsenal of flea repellents.

Fill small drawstring bags (available at cooking supply and natural foods stores) with fresh or dried chamomile leaves, walnut leaves, or cedar shavings, and tuck them into your dog's bedding (where they can't be chewed) to repel fleas.

Sprinkle garlic powder or mix a crushed garlic clove into your dog's food to ward off fleabites. Both garlic and chamomile are attractive flowering perennials, so for a free supply, try growing these herbs in your flower or vegetable beds.

A sprinkle of brewer's yeast (buy from health food stores) daily on your pets' food is also thought to help them repel fleas.

Soap kills fleas. When bathing your dog, begin by lathering the neck area and then work your way toward the tail, because fleas tend to congregate around the neck.

After rinsing, rub apple cider vinegar through the fur to help repel fleas, and add a teaspoon (5 ml) of cider vinegar to the dog's drinking water.

Mix Your Own Repellents

Homemade flea repellents are easy to mix and bottle, so why not give them a try? Use them to spritz your dog or cat almost all over, especially under the "armpits," behind the ears and around the head, taking care to shield the eyes. When you spray at the base of the tail, avoid spraying the pet's genitals. Two quick recipes:

Lemon Lash-Out Cut 2 lemons into small pieces, toss the pieces into a saucepan holding 1 quart (1 L) water, and boil the pieces for 1 hour. Remove pan from the heat and let the mixture stand overnight. Strain the lemony liquid into a spray bottle and spritz your pet as directed above.

Vinegar Vamooser Repel fleas with a solution made from 10 parts water to 1 part white vinegar. Pour it into a spray bottle and spray your pet as directed above.

END CARPET ODOR WITH BAKING SODA

If a musty smell has infiltrated the carpet, as often happens with recently cleaned pet urine spots, use baking soda to neutralize the odor. Once the carpet has thoroughly dried, sweeten the area by working ⅛ to ¼ cup (30 to 60 ml) baking soda into the carpet pile. Wait 15 minutes before vacuuming it up.

DE-SKUNK WITH VINEGAR

Many people have heard of using tomato juice to rid a pet's coat of skunk odor, but here's a less expensive and neater way to remove the scent: Deodorize your pet with a bath of 50:50 white vinegar and warm water. Keep rinsing and washing until all odor is gone. Your pet is a water-wary cat, you say? Consult cat care guides or browse the internet for ways to bathe a cat, which involve enlisting a helper, using a hand-held shower nozzle, staying patient and calm, and reassuring Missy repeatedly that it's going to be OK.

AWAY WITH PET HAIR!

Try vacuuming your pet, using the brush

attachment on your vacuum. If the pet doesn't mind the noise, make this a weekly task that will collect loose hairs before they start flying around the house. If your pet doesn't like being vacuumed, try holding the vacuum brush about 2 inches (5 cm) from its fur.

REVITALIZE DRY HAIR WITH TEA

If your pet's coat is looking a little less than lustrous, shampoo Fluffy or Fido as you usually do, then complete the wash by rinsing the coat with a quart (1 L) of warm unsweetened tea.

RECYCLE A SHOWER CURTAIN LINER

Covering your furniture with an old shower curtain is likely to keep pets at arm's length and your furniture cleaner. It isn't comfortable to lie on, and the crunchy plastic makes an unpleasant noise when your pet climbs onto it.

KEEP PET FOOD ANT-FREE

Placed on the floor, pet food bowls are like a natural magnet for ants. Here's a simple, totally nontoxic way to keep ants away. Set an empty pie plate where you usually feed your pet. Fill the pet's bowl with food and set it into the pie plate. Pour water into the pie plate, filling it to the rim. Ants and other crawling insects cannot cross this "moat" to the food. Another way to keep bugs away from your pets' dishes is to place a border of baking soda around their food bowls to keep away six-legged intruders. And it won't harm your pet if he happens to lap up a little (though most pets aren't likely to savor soda's bitter taste).

CLEAR THE AIR WITH COFFEE BEANS

Some pet owners remove pet odors from a room by heating a cup (250 ml) freshly ground coffee beans in a cast-iron skillet over low heat. As soon as the scent is released, remove the pan to the smelly

UNSTICK SOMETHING STICKY

That sticky something in your pet's fur could be pine sap, mud or something unmentionable. Before you get out the scissors and cut away the patch, leaving your dog or cat with a bald spot, try this: Mix 1 teaspoon (5 ml) mild shampoo or liquid dish detergent with ¼ to ½ cup (60 to 125 ml) warm water and whisk well. Wearing rubber gloves, apply some of the solution to the spot, rubbing it in with your fingers. Then comb the spot with a wire-toothed brush. Once you've removed the sticky stuff, wash away any soapy residue with fresh warm water.

room and set it on a trivet. By the time the ground beans cool, much of the pet odor should have dissipated.

Unmark Your Pet's Spots

When you're housetraining a puppy or kitten, it will often wet previously soiled spots. After you clean up the mess, it's essential to remove the scent from your floor, carpeting or couch. And nothing does that better than vinegar.

On a floor, blot up as much of the stain as possible, then mop with equal parts white vinegar and warm water. (On a wood or vinyl floor, test a few drops of vinegar in an inconspicuous area first, to make sure that it won't harm the floor's finish.) Dry with a cloth or paper towel.

For urine stains on carpets, rugs and upholstery, thoroughly blot the area with a towel or some rags, then pour a bit of undiluted vinegar over the spot. Blot it up with a towel, reapply the vinegar and let it air-dry. Once the vinegar dries, the spot should be completely deodorized.

FOR THE DOGS

GET FLEAS OUT OF THE DOGHOUSE

If your dog enjoys its doghouse, chances are fleas do, too. Keep fleas from infesting your pet's home by washing down the interior walls and floor every few weeks with a solution of salt water. Then, pour table salt around all the crevices of the doghouse to keep fleas out.

STAIN RELIEF FOR RUGS

Did your dog relieve itself on your priceless rug? Scoop up the mess, turn the rug over, place a bucket under the offending spot and pour water repeatedly—through the underside of the stain and into the bucket—until the spot is gone, making sure to check that color is not lost. Add vinegar to the water if needed, as acids can help set dyes. This method will clean the delicate fibers without the need for scrubbing.

USE OLIVE OIL ON BADLY MATTED HAIR

Loosen your dog's matted hair by rubbing a little olive oil into the knot. Then gently comb through the matted area with a wire brush until the brush's teeth glide smoothly through Lucy's coat.

BRUSH-AND-GO DRY DOG SHAMPOO

Save heaps by substituting this single ingredient for a commercial dry pet shampoo. Travel friendly! This makes 1 or more shampoos, depending on dog size.

1   box (1 lb. or 454 g) baking soda

Test for sensitivity by rubbing a little baking soda into the dog's coat between its ears (where it can't be licked off). Wait 5 minutes; check for reddening or other signs of irritation. If there are none, proceed.

Rub the baking soda into the dog's coat, working it in all the way to the skin. Avoid the eyes, nose, mouth and ears. Allow soda to remain in the coat for a full minute to absorb oil and odor.

Brush the fur with a pet brush until all baking soda and debris are removed.

REMOVE BAD SMELLS FROM A CURIOUS DOG

Is there a dog alive that hasn't rolled in something foul and stinky? If your dog does this, douse the affected area thoroughly with undiluted tomato juice. Be sure to sponge some of the juice over your pet's face, too, avoiding its eyes. Wait a few minutes for the acids from the tomatoes to neutralize the smell, then give your pet a shampoo or scrub with soap and water. Repeat as necessary over several days until the smell is completely gone.

PREVENT HAIR CLOGS

Stuff some steel wool in your bathtub drain the next time you wash your dog. It will prevent its hair from clogging the drain. Just make sure that you don't press the steel wool too far down; you'll want to remove it when you're done.

Remove Stinky Odors

If your dog has rolled in something unpleasant, here are a few more ways to help get rid of the smell:

Bathe your pet in a mixture of ½ cup (125 ml) white vinegar, ¼ cup (60 ml) baking soda and 1 teaspoon (5 ml) liquid soap in 1 quart (1 L) 3% hydrogen peroxide. Work the solution deep into its coat, give it a few minutes to soak in, then rinse the mixture out thoroughly with clean water.

Bathe your pet in equal parts water and vinegar (preferably outdoors), then repeat using 1 part vinegar to 2 parts water, followed by a good rinsing.

If cleaning the dog means you also get the smell on you, use undiluted vinegar to get the smell out of your own clothes. Let the affected clothing soak in the vinegar overnight.

CAT LOVERS

LITTER BOX HACK

Why clean a smelly plastic litter box when you can get biofriendly ones for free and toss them out, dirty litter and all? Make a habit of stopping by your local convenience store or beverage store and asking for their empty plastic-wrapped shallow boxes—the kind that hold a dozen cans of soft drink. Keep the plastic on the box while in use, then pull it off and toss it into the recycling bin before dumping the litter-filled box into the trash. This also makes for a convenient toss-and-go litter box for traveling.

GOODBYE, LITTER SMELLS

You love your cat, but you likely don't love its litter box. Luckily, you can use hydrogen peroxide to clean it and help get rid of the odor. You can put 3% hydrogen peroxide into a bottle and spray the sides, then pour some hydrogen peroxide into the bottom of the box. Let the litter box sit for 30 minutes, dump the remnants down the drain and wash the litter box with warm water.

NO-COST LITTER BOX CLEANER

Instead of using name-brand or off-brand cleaning products, choose one of these kitchen pantry or under-the-sink items to keep a litter box fresh as a daisy. After removing litter and liner, clean the box weekly with vinegar and lemon oil. Finish the job by rinsing the

RECIPE: DRY CAT SHAMPOO

Take the stress out of bath time for your cat with this soothing dry shampoo. You'll save pocket change, too, as it's made from pantry staples. This makes 1 shampoo.

- ⅓ **cup (80 ml) unprocessed bran**
- ⅓ **cup (80 ml) cornmeal**
- ⅓ **cup (80 ml) rolled oats**

Pour the grains into a microwave-safe container, seal, and shake to combine. Warm in the microwave on low for 10 seconds.

Rub the warm grains into your pet's fur. When finished, brush the grains out along with oil, dirt and dander.

litter box with plain water. Then wipe it dry with a clean cloth before refilling it.

BAKING SODA TRICK

Don't waste money on expensive deodorized cat litter; just put a thin layer of baking soda under the bargain-brand litter to absorb the odor. Or mix baking soda with the clean litter as you're changing it.

SWEETEN IT UP

If you're buying scented litter or the kind that neutralizes litter box odors, you're probably spending a lot every week on this kitty essential. A suggestion to help you achieve the same result at less expense? Stir a handful of dried parsley or other aromatic dried herb into the litter.

SLICE LEMON, NEUTRALIZE ODOR

Let's face it: There's nothing pleasant about eau de litter box—and here's a way to control odor in the area where the box sits. Place half a lemon, cut side up, on a saucer and set it on the floor a few inches from the box. (A scientist could explain to you why the smell of lemon in the air neutralizes unpleasant odors, but suffice it to say that lemon gives baking soda a run for the money when it comes to odor control.) For tough odors, place several lemon halves on a paper plate, or try a combo of orange, lemon and lime halves.

A DOORMAT FOR CATS

To keep your cat from tracking dusty paw prints on the floor when she leaves her litter box, place a carpet remnant or an old cloth place mat on the side of the box where Precious makes her exit.

STAY OUT, OR OFF

If you want to keep cats out of the kids' playroom, or discourage them from using your favorite easy chair as a scratching post, sprinkle some full-strength distilled white vinegar around the area or on the object itself. Cats don't like the smell of vinegar and will avoid it.

FOIL AS A NOISY DETERRENT

Noise deters pets from jumping onto furniture. To train cats to stay off upholstered couches and chairs, top the cushions with aluminum foil. If cats jump onto the furniture, the crunching sound of foil under their paws will send them scurrying in a hurry.

TIPS FOR FISH AND BIRD OWNERS

FISHY FISH TANK

To remove mineral deposits from hard water in your fish tank, rub the inside of the tank with salt, then rinse the tank well before reintroducing the fish. Use only plain, not iodized, salt.

PANTYHOSE TANK CLEANERS

Once you've removed the fish, the water and any ornaments from an aquarium tank, you can turn an old pair of pantyhose into a cleaning tool in two ways: 1) Fit a leg over your arm so you have the foot over your fingers, like a mitten. 2) Ball the pantyhose up and use it as you would a sponge. No matter which method you choose, make a simple vinegar and water solution (1 part white vinegar to 1 part water) and use pantyhose to wipe down the sides and bottom of the tank.

PUT AQUARIUM WATER TO GOOD USE

When you change the water in your tank, don't pour it down the drain! It's ideal for hatching brine shrimp (the favorite food of seahorses, if you keep a seahorse or two in your aquarium), and it makes an excellent fertilizer for houseplants and outdoor ornamentals alike. The nutrients in the water make flowering plants and vegetables thrive like few other fertilizers. And don't be put off by the smell—it will dissipate about an hour after you water your plants.

CLEANING HOUSE FOR BIRDS

A 50:50 mixture of water and white vinegar turns a birdcage into a sparkling clean home and does a good job of cleaning plastic bird toys. After wiping on the mixture, rinse with fresh water, then dry with a clean cloth.

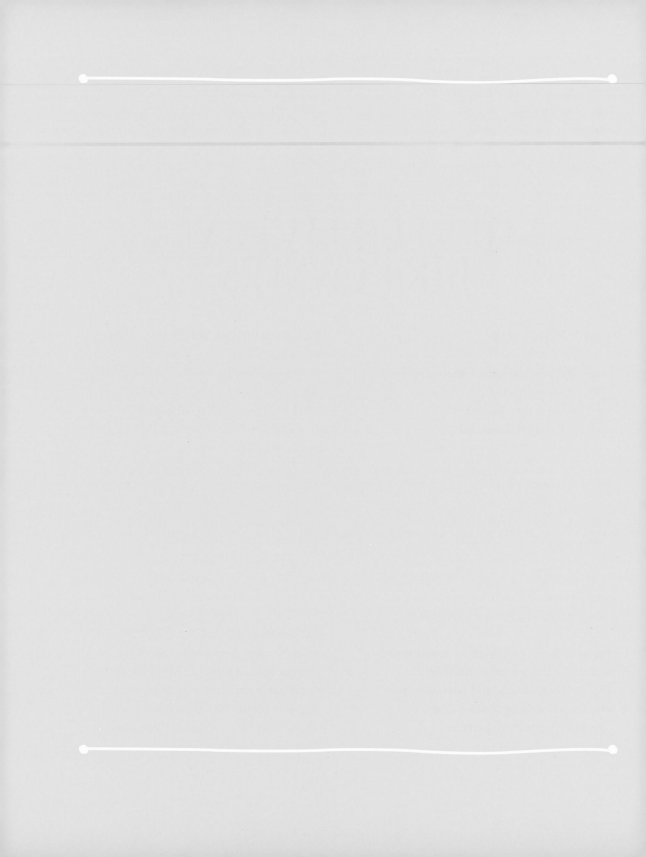

PERSONAL CARE

DIY BEAUTY PRODUCTS

Going Homemade

Some cosmetics contain harsh chemicals. Homemade beauty products take advantage of plant-based oils for moisture and essential oils for delightful scents. Here are some of the most popular natural ingredients you can use.

PLANT-BASED OILS

Almond oil is good to use for massages and to care for all skin types.

Apricot kernel oil makes an excellent massage oil and has a faint scent of almonds. It is appropriate for all skin types but is particularly good for dry, sensitive skin.

Avocado oil provides moisture, nourishment and hydration for the skin.

Evening primrose oil stimulates and improves the appearance of skin. It is also sometimes used in conditioners for brittle, overprocessed hair. Use it only in small amounts as it is extremely potent.

Jojoba oil, a liquid wax, controls moisture and doesn't leave an oily sheen on your skin. It's suitable for every skin type.

Macadamia nut oil is rich in fatty acids, making it an ideal ingredient for creams.

Olive oil nurtures every skin type but is especially suitable for dry, rough skin.

Rosehip oil is rich in essential fatty acids and provides ample moisture for rough skin. Use it only in small amounts—and only for scent, not as a base oil—as it is very strong.

Wheat germ oil is rich in vitamin E, which combats the aging of dry, mature skin.

ESSENTIAL OILS

Bergamot oil is the finest of all citrus oils, with a sweet, citrus-fresh scent.

Geranium oil provides a soft, flowery, feminine touch.

Jasmine oil is a highly aromatic oil with special softening and smoothing properties.

Lavender oil produces a pure, fresh, flowery scent used in many products.

Lemon oil spreads a pure, fresh scent with a subtle and sweet touch. It's ideal for cleansing.

Neroli oil gives a fresh, flowery scent with a touch of bittersweet orange.

Rose oil emanates a sweet, flowery scent with a very feminine oil.

Rosemary oil is an intense scent similar to camphor; use sparingly.

Sandalwood oil gives off a warm, heavy and long-lasting scent used by men and women.

Ylang-ylang oil exudes an exotic, sensual scent, ideal for perfume, deodorants and bath additives; use sparingly.

USEFUL INGREDIENTS

Beeswax gives creams, salves, lotions and lipsticks a thicker, more solid consistency.

Fruit or cider vinegar reduces itching, cools and refreshes. It regulates the pH value of skin,

cont. on p. 208

cont. from p. 207

acts as a natural antiseptic and promotes blood circulation. The vitamins and minerals that cider and fruit vinegars contain also make them ideal additives for cleansers and baths, but don't use malt, white or distilled vinegar in this way.

Cocoa butter melts at a low temperature and makes a good base for soaps and creams.

Glycerin is a clear, syrupy alcohol used as a lubricant in creams and lotions.

Lanolin—the pure oil from sheep's wool—is a moisturizing skin-care all-star, mostly due to its water-repellent properties.

Take Care

Plant-based fragrances can be risky: "Natural" doesn't necessarily equate to "safe." While essential oils can provide effective relief from colds, it's the dosage that makes them a poison, as there have been many cases of children suffering severe poisoning from essential oils. Always exercise great caution when using essential oils near children, and use them only as directed.

SAFETY FIRST

When you are sourcing and using natural ingredients, please keep these important advisories always in mind:

Be sure to use pesticide-free fresh plant materials—avoid collecting from roadside locations. Try not to get essential oils in your eyes or mouth, and avoid swallowing mouthwashes containing them. Some essential oils can cause changes in skin pigmentation in sunlight, so be sure to avoid applying before sun exposure. If you have allergies, check with your doctor before using any new ingredient. Patch-test homemade skin products before use by applying a small amount to the inner elbow, and then covering the spot. If there is no reaction after 24 hours, the product is safe for you to use.

BATH AND BODY

MILK DOES A BODY GOOD

Cleopatra knew the benefits of a milk bath for the skin, and some 2,000 years later, it's still true. Milk moisturizes and softens the skin. Pour 2 to 3 cups (500 to 750 ml) of milk into the bath as the water runs, or use a cup (250 ml) of powdered milk, and add a little scented bath oil. Soak for at least 10 minutes.

ADD SALT TO YOUR BATH

Most people have heard of bath salts, but usually this conjures images of scented crystals that bubble up in your tub and may contain coloring and other stuff that leaves bathtub rings behind. Now strip that picture to its core, and you've got

salt. Dissolve 1 cup (250 ml) table salt in your bathtub and soak as usual. Your skin will be noticeably softer. Buy sea salt for a real treat. It comes in larger chunks and can be found in health food stores or the gourmet section of supermarkets. You can also massage yourself with the dry salt just after a bath—while skin is damp.

SHAMPOO BUBBLE BATH

This recipe provides a scented, bubbly bath that's safe for your child and, as a bonus, helps you repurpose extra shampoo.

- ½ **cup (125 ml) shampoo**
- ¾ **cup (180 ml) water**
- ¼ **tsp. (1 ml) table salt**

In a medium bowl, mix the shampoo and water. Gently stir until blended. Add the salt. Stir until the mixture thickens.

Pour through a funnel into a clean bottle with a tight cap. This bubble bath will keep safely for months in the bathroom.

Discover the Joy of Bath Bags

Dress up these bath products with attractive cloth bags to create your own inexpensive bath goodies.

STRAWBERRIES AND CREAM BATH BAG

What a sweet treat for your body. The oatmeal mixture helps relieve dry skin. For extra-sensitive skin, reduce or eliminate the essential oil.

- ½ cup (125 ml) oats (regular or quick)
- ½ cup (125 ml) powdered milk
- 4 Tbsp. (60 ml) almond meal (if necessary, grind almonds in blender)
- 16 drops strawberry essential oil

In a small bowl, combine the oats, powdered milk and almond meal, stirring to mix well. Stir in the essential oil until blended. Divide mixture among 3 pretty cloth bags, and tie them closed at the top. Tie a generous loop of string or ribbon to the top of each bag.

When ready to use, hang the bag from the tub faucet by its loop.

When you fill the bath, the water will run over the mixture in the bag, dispersing it into the bath.

Keep the bath bags in a cool, dark place until ready to use.

HERBAL BATH BAG

This is a simple luxury for your bath. It makes you smell good afterward, but it is also delightful while you soak.

- 1 large handful mixed herbs (rosemary, lovage, lavender, lemongrass, sage, parsley or peppermint)
  Cheesecloth

Place the herbs of your choice in a doubled square of cheesecloth. Gather up the corners and tie them securely.

Toss herb bag into a hot bath to soften and scent the water. Once you're bathing, rub it over skin.

oil, use milk instead. Add a few drops of the oil to a little milk and spread it on your skin or use it in a bath. Make the solution fresh when you need it.

Insider Tip Got sprayed by a skunk? Wash with tomato juice. It's an old wives' tale that's also true.

SOAK IN A HOT TEA BATH

If a spot of tea in the afternoon is a calming break, a hot green tea bath in the evening after a tough day is a little touch of heaven. Place 2 tablespoons (30 ml) dried green tea leaves in the toe of an old nylon stocking, then bunch it up and close with a twist tie. Toss the bundle into a hot bath or tie it with string over the faucet opening so the water will run through. While you're enjoying the hot soak, the antioxidants of the tea will go to work, smoothing, soothing and calming you both outside and in.

HAVE A MILK MASSAGE

If you like to use essential oils for your personal fragrance but don't like the greasy feeling of the carrier

RECIPE: BASIC BATH POWDER

For an after-bath or after-shower touch, this fragrance-free homemade powder is so natural, it's a safe bet that your great-grandmother used it. Apply with a powder puff or sprinkle it on from a shaker-top jar.

½ cup (125 ml) baking soda
½ cup (125 ml) cornstarch

In a small bowl, stir the ingredients to combine. Store the bath powder in a wide-mouthed glass jar or keep in a shaker-top jar. The powder should keep indefinitely.

SCRUB ON A HEALTHY GLOW

You can spend a fortune on a sugar scrub at a salon—or you can mix ¼ cup (60 ml) olive oil with ¼ cup (60 ml) granulated sugar and use it like soap in the shower, scrubbing your arms, legs, shoulders and, gently, your face. Rinse well, pat dry and moisturize. You'll glow as if you just returned from a beach vacation! (This same mix will also safely scrub oil or paint off your hands.)

GINGER SNAPPER

Blend together equal amounts of freshly minced ginger and brown sugar, then add vanilla extract or sweet almond oil to make an energizing body scrub. Ginger contains valuable antioxidants and is known to stimulate circulation.

USE MILK FOR SHAVING

Use milk in place of shaving foam. Warm full-fat milk and pat it onto your skin. While you shave, continue to pat on more to keep your skin wet. For men, it's probably an emergency fix, but women shaving their legs may never go back!

TIGHTEN YOUR PORES WITH OATMEAL

Oatmeal makes an extremely soothing face mask that tightens your pores and leaves your skin feeling soft and smooth. Grind ¼ cup (60 ml) oatmeal to a fine powder in a blender. Add 1 egg white and 2 tablespoons (30 ml) honey. Pulse to combine, then smooth this mixture over your clean face, avoiding the eye area. Wear for 15 minutes, then rinse with warm water, pat dry and apply a light moisturizer.

KEEP VINEGAR IN THE SHOWER

Vinegar enthusiasts swear by apple cider vinegar instead of soap and shampoo for washing sensitive skin and rinsing chemical buildup from hair. Put a bottle of undiluted apple cider vinegar in the shower and see if it works for you, too.

Say Yes to a Relaxing Bath

Take advantage of the power of a long soak to soothe, moisturize and heal your skin. Once you have stepped out of the bath, be sure to apply a moisturizer.

FOR NORMAL SKIN

Open your pores with a yogurt-based bath additive. Puree a single-size serving plain yogurt, 1 tablespoon (15 ml) honey, 2 tablespoons (30 ml) almond oil and 1 vanilla bean in a blender. Add 10 drops of orange oil and swirl into bathwater.

Invigorate skin with a rosemary bath additive. Fill a small jar two-thirds full with fresh rosemary leaves, add enough sea salt to fill the jar, then fill with water. Let steep in a warm place for 2 weeks,

shaking vigorously every day. Put 2 tablespoons (30 ml) of the mixture in a cloth bag and add it to bathwater.

Pamper with a vanilla shower gel. Mix ½ cup (125 ml) neutral, unscented shampoo, ¼ cup (60 ml) warm water, a pinch of salt and 15 drops vanilla oil.

FOR OILY SKIN

Make a buttermilk bath by adding a puree made from 1 quart (1 L) buttermilk, juice of 4 lemons and 4 generous handfuls of peppermint leaves.

Soothe your skin with an oatmeal bath. Combine 1 cup (250 ml) oats, a handful each of fresh sage and peppermint leaves, and 10 drops of lemon oil in a cloth bag. Drop it in your bath, squeezing it occasionally.

cont. on p. 214

cont. from p. 213

Stimulate your body with a firming shower gel. Stir together 1 cup (250 ml) shower gel base (available from beauty supply stores or online) with 10 drops each geranium and lemon oils and 5 drops each rosemary, juniper and sage oils.

FOR MATURE AND DRY SKIN
Make skin silky-soft with a bath oil made from ¼ cup (60 ml) almond oil, 10 drops grapefruit oil, and 5 drops each lemon and orange oils.

Soak in a lavender bath. Cover a handful of dried lavender flowers with water, boil for 5 minutes and strain. Add 2 tablespoons (30 ml) honey and 1 tablespoon (15 ml) each cream, buttermilk and olive oil, and add mixture to bathwater.

CHAMOMILE SKIN TONER

If you have sensitive skin that feels dry and uncomfortable after washing with soap, try a facial toner with chamomile. Boil 4 cups (1 L) of water and soak 2 chamomile tea bags in it for 15 minutes. Discard the tea bags and cool the tea. Store in a glass jar in the fridge. To use, remove makeup with a soap-free remover, then soak several cotton balls in the cool tea and rub all over your face.

BANANA FACE MASK

Who needs Botox when you have bananas? That's right, you can use a banana as an all-natural face mask that moisturizes your skin and leaves it looking and feeling softer. Mash a medium-sized ripe banana into a smooth paste and gently apply it to your face and neck. Let sit for 10 to 20 minutes and rinse off with cold water. Another

cont. on p. 218

Make Your Own Soap

Follow these simple steps for soap making that will have you really looking forward to using it.

ALMOND ROSE SOAP

Here's a method of soap making that uses just a few basic tools. You'll create a fragrant soap that gently cleans and exfoliates.

2	Tbsp. (30 ml) dried red rose petals
2½	cups (625 ml) pure soap flakes
⅔	cup (160 ml) boiling water
½	cup (125 ml) rose water
2	Tbsp. (30 ml) ground almonds
9	drops geranium essential oil

Pound the rose petals with a mortar and pestle. In a large bowl, combine the ground petals, soap flakes and water and stir until smooth. If the soap starts to solidify, place the bowl over near-boiling water.

Stir in the rose water and ground almonds. Allow to cool. Stir in the essential oil.

Shape the mixture into 6 balls and flatten them slightly. Allow the soap to harden between sheets of parchment paper. Store unused soap in a cool, dark place.

DIY LIQUID OR GEL SOAP

This bath or hand soap is easy to cook up and is a good way to use up old slivers of bar soap.

2	cups (500 ml) pure soap flakes or grated bar soap
8	cups (2 L) water
2	Tbsp. (30 ml) glycerin

In a large pot or Dutch oven, combine all the ingredients. Cook over low heat, stirring occasionally, until the soap flakes have dissolved.

Transfer the mixture to a clean ½-gallon (2 L) container and cover tightly. For a thinner soap, increase water to 1 gallon (4 L).

Get a Natural Shave

Feel good during and after the shave with these green recipes.

ROSEMARY SHAVING SOAP

Rinse your face with fresh water, then lather up your beard with this fragrant soap before shaving. Rinse off the lather thoroughly.

- ⅔ **cup (160 ml) rose water**
- 1¼ **cups (310 ml) pure soap flakes**
- 4 **drops rosemary essential oil**
- 3 **drops lemon essential oil**
- 2 **drops bay essential oil**
- 1 **drop sage essential oil**

Warm the rose water in a nonreactive saucepan over low heat. Place the soap flakes in the top of a double boiler over simmering water. Stir the warmed rose water into the flakes to moisten. Keep stirring the mixture until the soap has melted to a smooth gel (if necessary, use a potato masher to dissolve the soap). Remove from the heat and cool to lukewarm.

Stir in the essential oils and spoon the soap into a sterilized shallow 7-ounce (210 ml) glass jar with a tight-fitting lid. Set aside to harden for 3 to 5 days. Keep handy in a cool, dark place.

ALOE AFTERSHAVE GEL

This alcohol-free gel is suitable for men or women because it refreshes and is safe for sensitive skin. Aloe vera gel is available in health food stores—or you can scoop it out of the leaves of a plant.

- ½ **cup (125 ml) aloe vera gel**
- 1½ **Tbsp. (22 ml) distilled water**
- 3 **tsp. (15 ml) witch hazel**
- 10 **drops essential or fragrance oils of your choice**

Combine all the ingredients in the container you're going to store the gel in. Stir until well mixed. Cover the container with a tight-fitting lid.

Keep in a cool, dark place. The gel should keep indefinitely.

LIGHTLY SCENTED AFTERSHAVE

Aftershave splashes serve two purposes: to soothe the just-shaved beard area and to offer a pleasant scent. Instead of purchasing costly scented aftershaves, make this at home for a fraction of the price.

½ cup (125 ml) witch hazel
½ cup (125 ml) rose water

Combine the witch hazel and rose water in a sterilized jar. Splash on your face directly after shaving. Keep mixture tightly covered. The aftershave should keep indefinitely.

DIY Chocolate Body Wrap
Love chocolate so much that you could bathe in it? Here's your chance.

Just warm ½ cup (125 ml) of honey in a microwave or the top of a double boiler. Then stir in 1½ cups (375 ml) of unsweetened cocoa until it dissolves. If the mixture cools, reheat it, but don't let it get hot.

Now spread the mudlike paste evenly over your body.

Here comes the good part: Wrap your legs, arms and torso in plastic wrap to seal in the paste and sit tight for 20 minutes.

That done, peel off the wrap and wash away the paste in a warm shower or bath. Your skin should feel silky smooth, thanks to the hydrating and revitalizing antioxidants in cocoa and honey. And all without a single calorie!

cont. from p. 214

popular mask recipe uses ¼ cup (60 ml) plain yogurt, 2 tablespoons (30 ml) honey and 1 medium banana, mixed together.

MINIMIZE WRINKLES WITH HONEY

Discourage wrinkling by applying a facial mask made of honey once a week, as Cleopatra did. Honey has properties that soften and hydrate skin and help it retain moisture, plus antioxidants and various compounds that can soothe irritations and inflammations. To make a honey mask, warm the honey. While it's heating, press a warm washcloth to your face to open pores. Carefully spread the honey around your face, keeping it away from the eyes. Relax 15 minutes, then

rinse, using cold water in the final rinse to close pores. Though skin may not look like a baby's, it should feel almost as soft.

LEMON CLEANSE YOUR FACE

Clean and exfoliate your face by washing it with lemon juice. You can also dab

CORNMEAL HAND SCRUB

This gentle massage scrub costs small change to make and leaves your hands smooth and soft.

- ¼ cup (60 ml) cornmeal
- 3 Tbsp. (45 ml) milk
- 1 drop almond oil (or almond extract)

In a small saucepan, mix the cornmeal with the milk. Heat the mixture over a low heat until it forms a paste. Remove from heat and stir in the almond oil. Allow to cool.

Spread the mixture on your hands and allow to sit for 10 minutes. Gently scrub your hands with the mixture and then rinse off with warm water.

lemon juice on blackheads to draw them out during the day. Your skin should improve after several days of using this treatment.

APPLE CIDER VINEGAR FOR SKIN

Using vinegar as a skin toner dates back to the time of Helen of Troy. And it's just as effective today. After washing your face, mix 1 tablespoon (15 ml) apple cider vinegar with 2 cups (500 ml) water as a finishing rinse to cleanse and tighten skin. You can also make your own facial treatment by mixing ¼ cup (60 ml) cider vinegar with ¼ cup (60 ml) water. Gently apply the solution to face and let it dry.

TWO-FOR-ONE HAIR AND SKIN

Condition your hair and smooth your

STRAWBERRY FOOT SCRUB

Can't get to the spa for a luxury treatment for those tired feet? Work this simple and sweetly scented natural scrub into your feet and feel like a queen.

2	tsp. (10 ml) coarse salt
2	Tbsp. (30 ml) olive oil
8	fresh strawberries

Pour salt into a mixing bowl. Add the oil and stir to combine. Hull the strawberries and slice or chop them. Add strawberries to the salt and oil mixture and mash with a potato masher or fork. The resulting mixture should be chunky but well blended.

Rub this mixture onto your feet, massaging the balls of the feet and the heels. If desired, use a body puff or foot brush. Rinse off and coat feet with a gentle lotion.

face at the same time with a mayonnaise treatment. Massage mayo into your dry hair and scalp, then wrap it in a towel or put on a shower cap. While your hair rests in this luxurious treatment, spread

Quick Guide: The Best Body Oil for Your Skin Type

To make body oil, put 4 teaspoons (20 ml) almond oil in a small sterile glass jar with a tight-fitting lid. Add the appropriate drops of essential oils listed here for your skin type, shake and apply. Each blend will give you 4 body rubs.

NORMAL SKIN
8 drops lavender
6 drops geranium
2 drops chamomile

DRY SKIN
8 drops patchouli
4 drops geranium
2 drops carrot

OILY SKIN
10 drops lemon
6 drops geranium
4 drops sandalwood

SENSITIVE SKIN
3 drops geranium
2 drops patchouli

a thin layer of mayo over your freshly washed face, avoiding the eye area. Lie down with a couple of damp tea bags or cucumber slices over your eyes for 15 minutes and then step right into the shower to wash it all off. You'll feel as if you're just back from the salon.

CLEAN AND SOFTEN DIRTY HANDS

Working in the garden usually results in stained and gritty hands. Regular soap just won't get it off, but this will. Make

a paste of rolled oats and milk and rub it vigorously on your hands. The stains will be gone, and the oats-and-milk mixture will soften and soothe your skin.

GOT GREASY, GRIMY HANDS?

To clean filthy hands of grease, grime or paint easily and thoroughly, pour equal amounts of olive oil and sugar into the cupped palm of one hand, and gently rub your hands together for several minutes. Rinse thoroughly and dry. The grit of the sugar acts as an abrasive to help the oil remove grease, paint and grime. Your hands will look and feel clean, soft and super moisturized.

NO MORE FOOD ODORS

The smell of garlic or fish can linger on your fingers long after the food is gone. Avoid that by scrubbing your wet hands with baking soda, just as if it were soap, then rinse in warm water. Your hands will smell sweet—and feel softer, too.

Handy Hack

Don't despair if you suddenly run out of deodorant. Swipe a little hydrogen peroxide under arms instead. You'll kill the bacteria that cause odors. Rubbing alcohol will work, too!

FRESHEN UP FEET WITH TEA

Sweaty, smelly feet ruining your shoes and your day? Every night, soak feet in a basin of strong tea for 20 minutes. After a week or two, you should notice a real difference in both the sweat output and the odor.

DIY DEODORANT

Here's a serious homemade underarm deodorant that really works and won't stain your clothes or strain your wallet.

- ¼ cup (60 ml) distilled witch hazel
- 1 oz. (30 ml) sage alcohol-based herbal extract
- 10 drops grapefruit-seed extract
- 10 drops clary sage essential oil
- 5 drops patchouli essential oil

In a small repurposed spray bottle, combine all ingredients.

Shake well and spray under arms as needed.

Sugar Without the Guilt!

Indulge in these sweet scrub recipes that will invigorate you.

DRY SKIN SUGAR SCRUB

This body scrub costs less than a cup of coffee for three or four uses.

- 1 cup (250 ml) sugar
- ½ cup (125 ml) olive, grapeseed or other oil
- 2 drops vanilla or almond extract (optional)

In a medium bowl, combine the sugar and oil. Mix with a wooden spoon until you achieve a paste-like blend. Add extract if desired and stir until incorporated.

Transfer to a clean, airtight glass container to slow oil breakdown.

In the shower, massage mixture gently over damp skin. It will exfoliate and moisturize at the same time. Do not use on broken, irritated or scarred skin. Avoid the eyes. This is an especially oily mixture, so it is best for dry skin.

Store in the refrigerator for 6 months to 1 year.

CRANBERRY SUGAR SCRUB

Offer up scent while exfoliating, nourishing and polishing the skin.

- ½ cup (125 ml) frozen cranberries
- 1 tsp. (5 ml) glycerin
- ¼ cup (60 ml) sweet almond oil
- ¼ cup (60 ml) sugar
- 2 drops orange essential oil
- 2 Tbsp. (30 ml) oat powder

In a food processor, combine the cranberries, glycerin and almond oil. Process for 30 seconds, without turning berries to pulp. Keep the mixture thick.

Transfer the mixture to a bowl and stir in the sugar. Stir in the essential oil. Add just enough of the oat powder to create a cohesive mixture that you can apply to your skin.

In the shower, rub the mixture on your skin. Massage in and remove with warm water.

6 Beauty Fixes with Lemon

Considering its size, the vitamin C powerhouse we know as the lemon provides an astonishing number of beauty benefits. (One word of caution: Lemons can cause skin to be extra-sensitive to sunlight, so don't expose yourself to the sun for too long after a skin treatment.)

1. Exfoliate dead skin and bring new skin to the surface by washing skin with lemon juice mixed with a little sugar.

2. Smooth wrinkles by boiling 1 cup (250 ml) milk, 2 teaspoons (10 ml) lemon juice and 1 tablespoon (15 ml) brandy. Cool the mixture to room temperature, apply and let dry before wiping it off.

3. Lighten age spots by dabbing them with lemon juice and rinsing off after 15 minutes. Repeat once later in the day.

4. Mix the juice from 1 lemon with ¼ cup (60 ml) olive oil or sweet almond oil for a facial that both exfoliates and moisturizes.

5. Fight dandruff with a daily scalp massage with 2 tablespoons (30 ml) lemon juice. Rinse with water and follow with a rinse of 1 cup (250 ml) water mixed with 1 teaspoon (5 ml) lemon juice.

6. Whiten and clean fingernails by soaking them in 1 cup (250 ml) lukewarm water and the juice of half a lemon for 5 minutes, then rub the inside of the lemon rind against the nails.

 Insider Tip

To get the most juice out of fresh lemons, bring them to room temperature and roll them under your palm on the kitchen counter before squeezing. This breaks down the connective tissue and juice-cell walls, releasing more liquid when you squeeze the lemon.

DIY Moisturizing

Use one of these refreshing methods to rejuvenate your skin.

CITRUS MOISTURIZING TREATMENT

Leave skin soft and silky while barely leaving a mark on your grocery bill.

- 1 **egg yolk**
- 2 **Tbsp. (30 ml) lemon juice**
- 1 **cup (250 ml) olive oil**

In a medium bowl, whisk the egg yolk, lemon juice and olive oil together until the mixture reaches a creamy consistency. Thin with more lemon juice as desired.

Massage into your skin as an intense moisturizing treatment before a shower or bath. Apply a light coating on your hands, arms, legs and face. Gently massage into nails and cuticles. Apply about 1 tablespoon (15 ml) to each foot. Gently massage your toes, one by one, and then the arch of your foot, moving to the heel. Relax and allow the moisturizer to soak in for 10 to 15 minutes. Wipe away the excess and then step into the shower or tub to complete the treatment.

Store any leftovers in the refrigerator for a day or two.

GREEN ALOE MOISTURIZING LOTION

It takes almost no time and very little money to cook up this delightful body lotion that has aloe vera, an antioxidant, as its primary ingredient.

- 1 **cup (250 ml) aloe vera gel**
- 1 **tsp. (5 ml) vitamin E oil (if necessary, break several 500 IU capsules)**
- 5 **to 10 drops essential oil of your choosing**
- ¾ **oz. (22 ml) cosmetic-grade beeswax, grated or shaved**
- ½ **cup (125 ml) vegetable oil**

In a medium bowl, stir together the aloe vera gel, vitamin E and essential oil. Set aside.

In the top of a double boiler over simmering water, melt together the beeswax and vegetable oil. Stir until smooth and well blended. Remove from heat.

Slowly and continuously pour the melted mixture into the bowl with the aloe vera mixture, using a handheld electric mixer at slow speed to combine. Run a clean rubber spatula around the rim of the bowl to incorporate all the ingredients. Continue mixing until all the ingredients are blended.

Pour the final mixture into one sterilized 13-ounce (385 ml) jar or two sterilized 6-ounce (180 ml) jars with tight-fitting lids. You can use sterilized jam jars if you have them. Keep the lotion in the refrigerator for up to 6 weeks.

Serve Yourself a Yogurt Facial

You don't have to go to a spa. Just grab some yogurt from the fridge.

To cleanse your skin and tighten pores, slather plain yogurt on your face and let it sit for about 20 minutes, then rinse clean.

For a revitalizing face mask, mix 1 teaspoon (5 ml) plain yogurt with the juice from a quarter slice of orange, some of the orange pulp and 1 teaspoon (5 ml) aloe vera. Leave on your face at least 5 minutes before rinsing thoroughly.

Splash Power!

Refresh with these scents morning, noon or night.

SUMMER BODY SPLASH

A delicate mixture of fruit and flower scents will be just perfect for hot summer days and nights.

- ⅓ cup (80 ml) vodka
- 10 drops lavender essential oil
- 5 drops lime essential oil
- 5 drops lemon essential oil
- 5 drops lemongrass essential oil
- 2 cups (500 ml) distilled or boiled, cooled water

Pour the vodka and essential oils into a sterilized 20-ounce (600 ml) bottle with a tight-fitting stopper. Stopper the bottle and shake for several minutes. Add the distilled or boiled water and shake for several minutes more. Set aside for at least 48 hours or up to 3 weeks.

Place a paper coffee filter in a sieve and drip the liquid through the filter into a ceramic or glass bowl. Pour the liquid back into the large bottle or into a few smaller sterilized bottles. Keep one bottle in the refrigerator and store the others in a cool, dark place until needed.

CITRUS COLOGNE SPLASH

Make this cooling scent at home for spare change.

- 1 lime
- ½ cup (125 ml) rubbing alcohol
- 3 tsp. (15 ml) lemon extract or orange extract

Juice the lime and strain out the pulp. Combine the rubbing alcohol, lime juice and lemon or orange extract in a clean bottle with a tight-fitting lid. Shake well.

Dab on pulse points. You may also transfer the splash to a repurposed spray bottle. Store the splash in the refrigerator.

HAIR SITUATION

A QUICK, SWEET-SMELLING VINEGAR HAIR RINSE

Pick up a bottle of raspberry or plum vinegar next time you go shopping. It's inexpensive in the supermarket and it can do double duty in the kitchen. Use some for salad dressings but save a few spoonfuls for this recipe. Rather than prepare this rinse ahead of time, simply bring a clean 1- or 2-cup (250 or 500 ml) measuring cup containing 2 to 3 tablespoons (30 to 45 ml) scented vinegar into the shower. After you've shampooed, add water and rinse your hair with the solution. You can use this every time you shampoo if you like. Vinegar restores the proper acidic pH balance to hair. This rinse will remove remnants of shampoo and give your hair more shine.

MAINTAIN DARK, GLOSSY HAIR

To keep black, brown and chestnut hair glossy, rinse weekly with an herbal tea of color-enhancing spices and herbs. In 3 cups (750 ml) of boiling water, steep 1 teaspoon (5 ml) each of dried rosemary, sage, cinnamon and allspice, along with ½ teaspoon (2.5 ml) ground cloves. Strain through a paper towel-lined sieve or a coffee filter and let cool. Use as the final rinse after washing your hair.

LIGHTEN UP!

For blond hair, use 1 tablespoon (15 ml) chamomile. Pour 1 cup (250 ml) boiling water over the herb, steep for 30 minutes and then strain through a coffee filter. Cool. Pour repeatedly over your hair (and into a large bowl) as a final rinse after shampooing.

REPAIR DAMAGED STRANDS

Too much sun, chemicals, blow-drying and curling can leave hair as dry and brittle as autumn leaves. Put hair in a time machine and undo severe damage with olive oil. Wash hair and rinse with warm water. Heat ½ cup (125 ml) of olive oil in the microwave for about

45 seconds, until it's warm but you can still hold your finger in it. Massage it all through your hair and then cover your hair with an old shower cap. Cover with a towel and wear it for 30 minutes. Shampoo and rinse well, and your hair will feel thick and silky.

RECIPE: THICK HAIR CONDITIONER FOR EVERYONE

This two-ingredient conditioner offers a protein boost for your hair that in turn will make it feel thicker and more luxuriant. You don't need to go to an expensive hair salon to revitalize your hair.

- ½ ripe avocado
- ¼ cup (60 ml) coconut milk, or as needed

In a small bowl, mash the avocado with a spoon. Mix in the coconut milk to form a thick gel-like substance.

Apply entire recipe to clean hair and comb through. Leave the conditioner on the hair for 10 to 15 minutes. Rinse thoroughly.

GIVE YOURSELF A HOT-OIL TREATMENT

You don't need a spa or special oils for silky hair! An alternative to olive oil is to heat ½ cup (125 ml) of vegetable oil in the microwave for 20 seconds until it's just warm. Massage into your dry scalp and hair and wrap in a towel for 10 minutes. Wash as usual.

BUTTER WORKS WONDERS FOR DRY HAIR

Return to the glossy tresses you had before all that blow-drying. Smooth and soften the cuticles of your hair with a superrich butter treatment. Rub a handful of soft butter into dry hair, working it gently down to the ends. Wrap your hair in a towel or put on a shower cap and leave in for 30 minutes. Wash and rinse thoroughly, and run your fingers through your luxurious tresses.

Handy Hack

Need a hair degrease? If your locks aren't looking so lovely, try mixing a dollop of dishwashing liquid into your shampoo. It fights grease in hair as well as on dishes!

REMOVE BUILT-UP GEL, HAIR SPRAY OR CONDITIONER

When it comes to personal grooming,

How Herbs Help

When it comes to a hair rinse, choose your herbs wisely.

Chamomile will keep scalp and hair follicles healthy.

Comfrey soothes scalp irritations.

Elderberries are traditionally used to add color to gray hair.

Lemongrass tones the scalp.

Nettle is an astringent that helps relieve skin irritations and itching.

Parsley will help relieve any skin irritations.

Rosemary is believed to enhance color of dark hair and help control dandruff.

Sage is an astringent for oily hair and benefits damaged or fragile hair.

Thyme has antiseptic, tonic and astringent properties.

Yarrow acts as a tonic for the hair.

too much of a good thing can spell bad news for your hair. But a thorough cleansing with baking soda at least once a week will wash all of the gunk out of your hair. Simply add 1 tablespoon (15 ml) baking soda to your hair while shampooing. In addition to removing all the chemicals you put in your hair, it will wash away water impurities and may even lighten your hair.

SUPER (BOWL) HAIR

If you have a six-pack of beer left over from your Super Bowl party, use a little to make a hops shampoo that gives your hair body, shine and volume. In an enamel-lined saucepan set over medium heat, bring ¾ cup (180 ml) beer to a boil, then simmer briskly until it reduces to ¼ cup (60 ml). Cool, then mix with 1 cup (250 ml) of your regular shampoo. Transfer it to a jar with a lid, and shake before using.

USE BEER AS SETTING RINSE

Put life back into flat hair with some flat beer. Before you get into the shower, mix 3 tablespoons (45 ml) beer in ½ cup (125 ml) warm water. After you shampoo your hair, rub in the solution, let it sit for a couple of minutes and rinse it off. When you see the result, you'll want to keep a six-pack in the bathroom!

DIY HIGHLIGHTING

Try this rich hair dressing that provides both sheen and elegance to tired-looking hair. It can also be used as a pressing solution for hair straightening.

> Juice of 1 lemon
> 2 tsp. (10 ml) chamomile tea

In a small bowl, mix the lemon juice and tea. To achieve blond highlights, use an inexpensive straw hat with lots of holes in it. Pull strands of hair you would like to lighten through the holes with a crochet hook or pencil.

Douse the strands with the mix. Sit in the sun for 1½ hours, using sunscreen on yourself, of course.

BANISH CHLORINE GREEN HAIR

Any blonde—whether natural or not—knows that too much time in the pool can leave a distinct green cast on light-colored locks, not to mention a decided smell of chlorine that builds up after days at the pool. To return tresses to their rightful color and eradicate the chlorine, massage ketchup into wet hair while in the shower and leave it for 10 minutes. Rinse well and shampoo as usual. The green will be gone, and you'll smell like nothing but freshly washed hair.

Handy Hack

Need a simple fix when blond hair turns green after someone swims in a pool with too much chlorine? Rinse the hair with club soda and it will return to its original color.

PROTECT BLOND HAIR BEFORE SWIMMING

Keep your golden locks from turning green before getting in a chlorinated pool by rubbing ¼ cup (60 ml) cider vinegar into your hair. Let it sit for 15 minutes before diving in.

PAINT VS. HAIR

It's not that difficult to get almost as much paint in your hair as you do on the walls during a big paint job. Luckily, you can easily remove that undesirable tint by moistening a cotton ball with some olive oil and gently rubbing it into your hair. The same approach is also effective for removing mascara—just be sure to wipe your eyes with a tissue when you're done.

GET GUM OUT OF HAIR

It's inevitable—kids get chewing gum in their hair. Put the gummy hair section in a bowl with some cola. Let soak for a few minutes, then rinse. Another option is to apply some peanut butter to the wad and rub the gum until it comes out. Your child's hair may smell like peanut butter until you shampoo it, but it's better than having to cut the gum out.

SHAMPOO SOMEONE WHO'S BEDRIDDEN

Oatmeal and baking soda make an excellent and effective dry shampoo that can be very comforting for someone who's bedridden or ill. It soaks up excess oils and neutralizes odors. Grind ¼ cup (60 ml) oatmeal to a fine powder in a blender, then add ¼ cup (60 ml) baking soda and pulse to combine. Put a towel around the shoulders of the person to be shampooed and another towel on the lap. Sprinkle a few tablespoons (30 to 45 ml) of this mixture over the scalp, working it to the roots with your fingers. Let it sit for 5 minutes, then gently brush it out over the towels.

INSTANT DRY SHAMPOO

Another dry shampoo that will do the job: Take 1 tablespoon (15 ml) of cornmeal or cornstarch and sprinkle the powder into the hair; massage it in section by section and comb out any tangles. Brush well to remove all the powder, stopping often to shake out the brush. The powder absorbs dirt and excess oil, leaving hair clean and shiny.

CONDITION HAIR NATURALLY

Want to put the life back into limp or damaged hair? You can whip up a terrific hair conditioner by combining 1 teaspoon (5 ml) apple cider vinegar with 2 tablespoons (30 ml) olive oil and 3 egg whites. Rub the mixture into your hair, and keep it covered for 30 minutes using a shower cap. Shampoo and rinse as usual.

CONTROL THAT DANDRUFF

To get dandruff under control, wet your hair and rub a handful of baking soda vigorously into your scalp. Rinse thoroughly and dry. Do this every time you normally wash your hair, but use only baking soda, not shampoo. Your hair may dry out at first, but after a few

DIY DANDRUFF TREATMENT

Over-the-counter dandruff treatments can be costly. You can create this herbal remedy for considerably less than you'll pay for a commercial treatment.

2	tsp. (10 ml)	dried rosemary
2	tsp. (10 ml)	dried thyme
⅔	cup (160 ml)	boiling water
⅔	cup (160 ml)	cider vinegar

Place the herbs in a heatproof ceramic bowl. Pour in the boiling water. Cover and allow to steep for 15 to 20 minutes.

Strain the liquid into a clean 10-ounce (300 ml) repurposed bottle with a tight-fitting lid. Add the vinegar and shake. Store in a cool, dark place.

After shampooing, rinse hair thoroughly and then massage a small amount of the herbal treatment into the scalp. Between shampoos, massage a small amount into the scalp before going to bed.

weeks your scalp will start producing natural oils, leaving your hair softer and free of flaking skin.

SAFE WAY TO KILL HEAD LICE

Dermatologists may recommend using mayonnaise to kill and remove head lice from kids instead of toxic over-the-counter preparations. What's more, lice are becoming more resistant to such chemical treatments. To treat head lice with mayonnaise, massage a liberal amount into the hair and scalp before bedtime. Cover with a shower cap to maximize the effect. Shampoo in the morning and use a fine-toothed comb to remove any lice and nits. To completely eradicate the infestation, repeat the treatment in 7 to 10 days.

CLEAN YOUR BRUSHES

Hairbrushes and combs should be washed periodically to remove the hair oils that build up. Remove any hair, then fill a sink with warm water and stir in a couple of spoonfuls of baking soda. Let the brushes and combs soak several hours, then rinse and air dry. (Some high-end brushes or those with a wooden base should not be soaked.)

NATURAL HEAD LICE TREATMENT

Try this herbal remedy for an effective, gentler alternative to harsh over-the-counter treatments.

- ¼ **cup (60 ml) olive oil**
- 20 **drops tea tree oil**
- 15 **drops rosemary essential oil**
- 15 **drops lemon essential oil**
- 15 **drops thyme essential oil**
  Small amount of regular shampoo (any kind)

Combine the olive oil and essential oils in a small bowl, add a small amount of shampoo and mix well.

Massage into dry hair, making sure it is thoroughly covered.

Cover the hair with a towel, plastic wrap or a shower cap and leave for 1 hour.

Shampoo the mixture out of the hair, then comb the hair carefully with a nit comb to remove any dead lice and nits.

MOUTH HYGIENE

DIY TOOTHPASTE

Adjust the ingredients to your liking and you'll be able to keep a family of four supplied with toothpaste for a whole year for less than the cost of one commercial tube.

- ½ cup (125 ml) baking soda
- 2 tsp. (10 ml) salt
- 3 tsp. (15 ml) glycerin
- 10 or more drops peppermint or wintergreen flavoring
  Warm water

In a small bowl, mix the baking soda and salt. Add the glycerin and flavoring. Add warm water, a drop at a time, until the texture and consistency seem right. Spoon the mixture into a clean squeeze bottle or any convenient clean container with a tight lid.

You may have to adjust the amount of glycerin to arrive at a consistency that suits you. This toothpaste will keep indefinitely in a covered container.

STOP BAD BREATH

Kill the bacteria that cause bad breath by storing your toothbrush in hydrogen peroxide. Stick it head down in a plastic container filled with the liquid, rinsing it thoroughly before every use.

TOOTHBRUSH CLEANING TRICK

Keep toothbrushes squeaky clean by immersing them in a solution of ¼ cup (60 ml) baking soda and ¼ cup (60 ml) water. Let brushes soak overnight about once every week or two. Make sure you give them a good rinsing before using.

A FAST, HARD-WORKING MOUTHWASH

For fighting bacteria and removing food particles caught in your teeth, this inexpensive solution is about as effective a mouthwash as you can get. It uses the standard 3% hydrogen peroxide sold in pharmacies. Hydrogen peroxide, however, may irritate sensitive teeth or delicate tissue in the mouth, so this rinse should not be used any more than three times a week. In a cup, mix 2 tablespoons (30 ml) hydrogen peroxide solution with 2 tablespoons (30 ml) water. Swish the mixture in your mouth for 30 seconds, then spit it out—don't swallow it.

Bad Breath? Good News.

If you've failed the breath test and people back away when you stop to chat, rely on these remedies from the garden to freshen your breath quickly.

Use this mouthwash regularly after brushing your teeth: Add 2 drops of chamomile, peppermint, clary sage or lemon balm oil to a glass of water and rinse your mouth with it, but avoid swallowing it.

For persistent bad breath, chew fresh parsley or mint leaves—both will freshen breath in an instant.

Mix together dill, anise and fennel seeds and chew a few of them occasionally.

If stomach problems are what are causing your bad breath, you could try this old and trusted home remedy: Chew on a coffee bean, which will neutralize the acid smell. But be sure not to swallow it.

Apples are a healthy snack that taste good and freshen breath.

When you're on the go, suck on a peppermint or eucalyptus candy.

Insider Tip

People who eat yogurt regularly are less prone to halitosis than people who don't.

FRESHEN YOUR BREATH THE OLD-FASHIONED WAY

Store-bought mouthwash can contain food coloring, alcohol and sweeteners, and it isn't cheap. Use this method and your breath will be just as sweet. Mix 1 teaspoon (5 ml) salt and 1 teaspoon (5 ml) baking soda into ½ cup (125 ml) water. Rinse and gargle. The baking soda will neutralize odors on contact. When used as a mouthwash, baking soda will also relieve pain from a mouth ulcer.

JUST ATE GARLIC?

After eating garlic or onions, a quick and easy way to sweeten your breath is to rinse your mouth with a solution made by dissolving 2 tablespoons (30 ml) apple cider vinegar and 1 teaspoon (5 ml) salt in a glass of warm water.

CLEAN DENTURES OVERNIGHT

If you're away from home and you forgot denture cleaner, don't panic. Instead, soak dentures overnight in a coffee mug topped off with club soda. The fizzy bubbles will lift away food particles and leave dentures feeling clean in the morning.

Home Remedies for Brushing Teeth

If you are looking for an alternative to over-the-counter toothpastes, try your hand at making one of these for your gum health.

For a gum-refreshing tooth powder, finely grate 8 teaspoons (40 ml) dried orange peel and mix with about 2 tablespoons (30 ml) dried peppermint leaves and 2 teaspoons (10 ml) sea salt. Store in a screw-top container. When brushing your teeth, just sprinkle a little powder on a moistened toothbrush.

To make a tooth powder for sensitive teeth and gums, mix together ¼ cup (60 ml) powdered arrowroot, 1 tablespoon (15 ml) cornstarch, 1 tablespoon (15 ml) fine kitchen salt and 5 drops each cinnamon, myrrh and clove essential oils. Sift to remove lumps; store in a china or glass jar with a tight-fitting lid. To use, press a moistened toothbrush into the mixture.

You can also keep your gums healthy by rubbing them with the inside of a lemon skin. Alternatively, brush your teeth occasionally with warm sage tea.

Refreshing Rinses
Keep it clean with a hint of flavor. Your mouth will thank you!

SIMPLY CLEAN MOUTHWASH

For just a few cents, you can cook up a potful of this rinse that tastes good and can be safely used as often as you like. Unlike more expensive commercial mouthwashes, it has no alcohol.

1   cup (250 ml) water
2   Tbsp. (30 ml) angelica seeds
    Dash of peppermint oil or lemon verbena

In a small saucepan over medium heat, bring the water to a boil. Remove from the heat. Stir in the angelica seeds and peppermint oil or lemon verbena. Let the mixture sit for 10 minutes. Strain off and discard the solids.

Store the liquid in a clean, covered container in the refrigerator and use every day. It should keep indefinitely.

ROSE FLOWER MOUTHWASH

Everything will be coming up roses with this breath freshener.

4   Tbsp. (60 ml) rose flowers
3   Tbsp. (45 ml) sage leaves
1   Tbsp. (15 ml) strawberry leaves
⅔   cup (160 ml) cider vinegar
½   cup (125 ml) rose water

Mix herbs in a sealable container and pour heated cider vinegar over the top.

Steep for 10 days, strain, then wring out herbs well.

Mix the remaining liquid with rose water and pour through a filter.

Add a dash to a glass of water and rinse.

Homemade Mouthwashes

Using mouthwash after brushing leaves your mouth fresh and clean. Here are some more natural options to try.

To make a pleasant-smelling, refreshing mouthwash, mix ¼ cup (60 ml) each water and vodka and 3 drops each of eucalyptus, anise and clove oils in a small bottle. Add 1 teaspoon (5 ml) of the mouthwash to a glass of water and gargle.

For another refreshing rinse, mix 2 cups (500 ml) vodka, 2 teaspoons (10 ml) peppermint oil, ½ teaspoon (2.5 ml) cinnamon oil and ¼ teaspoon (1 ml) anise oil. Add a dash to a glass of water; rinse.

To make a mouthwash that will help keep gums healthy, mix 2 teaspoons (10 ml) each arnica, propolis and sage tinctures. Add 10 drops of the mixture to a glass of water and rinse.

BAKING SODA ALONE

If you run out of your usual toothpaste, or if you're looking for an all-natural alternative to commercial toothpaste, just dip your wet toothbrush in some baking soda and brush and rinse as usual. You can also use baking soda to clean mouthpieces and dentures. Use a solution of 1 tablespoon (15 ml) baking soda dissolved in 1 cup (250 ml) warm water. Let the object soak for 30 minutes and rinse well before using.

INDEX

NOTES

_____

_____

_____

_____

_____

_____

_____

_____

_____

                        _____

                        _____

                        _____

                        _____

                        _____

MY CLEANING CHECKLIST

- ☐ _____
- ☐ _____
- ☐ _____
- ☐ _____
- ☐ _____
- ☐ _____
- ☐ _____
- ☐ _____
- ☐ _____
- ☐ _____
- ☐ _____
- ☐ _____
- ☐ _____
- ☐ _____
- ☐ _____
- ☐ _____

- ☐ _____
- ☐ _____
- ☐ _____
- ☐ _____
- ☐ _____
- ☐ _____
- ☐ _____
- ☐ _____
- ☐ _____
- ☐ _____
- ☐ _____
- ☐ _____
- ☐ _____
- ☐ _____
- ☐ _____
- ☐ _____